Great Texas Chefs

Great Texas
Chefs

by Judy
Alter

TCU PRESS • FORT WORTH
A TEXAS SMALL BOOK ★

Library of Congress Cataloging-in-Publication Data

Alter, Judy, 1938-
Great Texas Chefs / Judy Alter. -- 1st ed.
p. cm. -- (Texas small books)
ISBN 978-0-87565-377-8 (case : alk. paper)
1. Cooks--Texas. 2. Cookery. 3. Cookery--Texas. I. Title.
TX649.A1A48 2008
641.5092--dc22

2008008705

TCU Press
P. O. Box 298300
Fort Worth, Texas 76129
817.257.7822
http://www.prs.tcu.edu

To order books: 800.826.8911

Photo Credits: Messina Hof Winery & Resort, Courtesy of Bright Sky Press; *Brennan's of Houston*, Courtesy of Bright Sky Press; Chuck Wagon Cooks, Courtesy of Bright Sky Press; Helen Corbitt, Courtesy, *Fort Worth Star-Telegram*, Special Collections, University of Texas at Arlington Library, Arlington, TX; Courtesy of Lanny Lancarte; Courtesy Tim Love; Chad Martin, Courtesy Hôtel St. Germain; Recipes and photos from *Martinez Mex Tex; Traditional Tex-Mex Taste*, Courtesy Bright Sky Press; Courtesy of Stephan Pyles; Courtesy of Fonda San Miguel; Terry Thompson-Anderson, Courtesy of Shearer Publishing.

Recipes from: *Barbecue, Biscuits & Beans*, by Cliff Teinert, Bill Cauble, Tommy Lee Jones, & Watt Mathews Casey, Jr. (Bright Sky Press, 2002); *The Best from Helen Corbitt's Kitchens*, ed. Patty Vineyard MacDonald. (UNT Press, 2000); Jon Bonnell; Dean Fearing; *Fonda San Miguel*, by Tom Gilliland, Miguel Ravago & Virginia B. Wood. (Shearer Publishing, 2005); *The Kitchen Table*, by Randy Evans and Jay Stevens. (Bright Sky Press, 2006); Lanny Lancarte; Courtesy of Chad Martin, Hôtel St. Germain; *Martinez Mex Tex* by Matt Martinez and Mark Davis (Bright Sky Press 2006); Stephan Pyles; *Texas on the Plate* by Terry Thompson-Anderson (Shearer Publishing, 2002); *Vineyard Cuisine* by Merrill Bonarrigo and Paul Bonarrigo (Bright Sky Press, 2007).

Dedication

For Betty, who explores restaurants with me.

Contents

An Apologia of Sorts

More than one person will say, "How could you leave out so-and-so and include such-and-such," (supply any combination of names). The selections in this small book are based on several considerations, prime among them limited space. I also tried for a variety of cuisines and locales (living in Fort Worth, I could easily fill these pages with great food in my city, but this is a Texas book, not a Fort Worth one).

Some may question the inclusion of a vineyard, but the Bonarrigos have a classy cookbook, and I'm intrigued by both the combination of resort and vineyard and the Old World touch to the recipes.

And remember, like all the TCU Press Small Texas Books, *Great Texas Chefs* is written in a spirit of fun and enjoyment and, in this case, a clear love for really good food.

So send your complaints, suggestions, even praise, to me at Box 298300. Who knows? Maybe someday there'll be a *Great Texas Chefs II*.

~Judy Alter

Merrill and Paul Bonarrigo

Messina Hof Winery & Resort, Bryan

Vineyard Cuisine: Thirty Years of Meals and Memories from Messina Hof

MERRILL AND PAUL BONARRIGO AREN'T REALLY CHEFS—they are winemakers with a wonderful restaurant and resort and pioneers in bringing wine pairing to Texas. Wine culture is relatively new to the state—the Spaniards brought grapes in the sixteenth century, and these probably became the plentiful wild grapes that are found in rivers and streams and along roads and fences. But there was little history of winemaking until experimental vineyards started in the twentieth century at a very few places in the state. T. V. Munson, called the Grape Man of Texas, helped save the French wine industry when an insect infestation threatened the vineyards. Munson transplanted resistant stock from Texas to create a French/Texas hybrid. But Texans didn't seriously start growing wine until the 1970s, and then there were lots of jokes about bad Texas wines.

But to the Bonarrigos, wine is no joke. Merrill Mitchell Bonarrigo is a native of Bryan, Texas, and as a teenager baked for her family and dreamed one day of owning a bakery. Her maternal grandmother came from Hof, Germany, where Merrill's great-grandfather had been a baker.

Paul Bonarrigo grew up in the Bronx in a family for whom wine culture is a tradition. The family traces back to a village in the hills above Messina, Sicily, where his family were winemakers. His grandfather, Paul IV, brought the tradition to this country but could not follow his dream to plant grapes because of Prohibition. He made wine for the family from grapes trucked in from California. In later years Paul and his father joined Paul IV in winemaking.

It was natural that Paul, stationed in California with the U.S. Navy during the Vietnam War, took viticulture classes at the University of California/Davis and the Napa Wine School. Transferred from California to Florida, he drove through Texas and was amazed at the warm welcome he received as a serviceman. Discharged and having completed his physical therapy training at Columbia University, he returned to Texas.

Merrill was selling real estate and had a California client who wanted a contemporary house. She found three in Bryan and called the owners to see if they would consider selling. Two refused; Paul agreed to let her show his house if she could control his boxer, Sonny. She tried but couldn't, the clients were scared away, and she not only lost a sale, she didn't hear from Paul again.

Until two years later when he wanted to put his house on the market and called her. He took her to dinner and they fell in love. After their wedding, they knew they wanted land to grow grapes. In 1977 they began with a hundred acres and all the troubles that beset city folk when they first try to be farmers. Paul was busy with patients, so Merrill did much of the physical work, driving the tractor (often on an incline), planting the vines—one farmer told her he was sure those little sticks in the ground were dead. They were then one of only four wineries in the state.

Using grapes from other vineyards, they submitted wines to the State Fair of Texas and in 1981 their Cabernet Sauvignon won a gold medal. (They were then growing grapes for cabernet and chenin blanc but have since phased out of everything but the Lenoir grapes.) That same year they bought a second vineyard and by 1983 were ready for their first harvest. By then they had a son, young Paul, and all three were out in the vineyard early in the morning to harvest— only to find mockingbirds had eaten all their grapes. Soon, though, they were inviting international students from Texas A&M University to help with the harvest—most were students from European countries where wine-growing is a tradition. They missed the annual harvest tradition, with its food and camaraderie. The event grew so large that by 1993 harvesting was by invitation only.

The Bonarrigos bought a former Ursuline Academy building in 1982 and had it moved brick by brick to the vineyard. Senior architecture students from A&M submitted plans for building the resort they envisioned. The Villa, filled with the Bonarrigo's collection of family heirlooms and antiques and decorated by Merrill and her sister, opened October 28, 1999.

For years the Bonarrigos had been hosting dinner parties to showcase their wine. In 1996, they opened the Vintage House Restaurant. Early in their marriage Paul took Merrill to New York to meet his family, particularly Nona Bonarrigo, grandmother and matriarch of the family and her clan. Paul and Merrill were sent to Arturo's bakery and the Arthur Avenue market for supplies, and then Nona allowed Merril to assist her in the kitchen. They made antipasto, dandelion salad, spaghetti sauce, veal cutlets (forty of them), and dressed raw clams. Merrill thought the whole neighborhood was coming to dinner, at least forty people. There were five. But many of those dishes show up today at the Villa.

The cuisine is also inspired by their years of food and wine pairing, trips to Europe, and experiences with guest chefs. Executive Chef Ken Ruud, with experience in New Orleans and the Hamptons of New York, presides over a menu that uses the fresh vegetables and herbs grown on the estate. There is a Messina Hof wine in every dish. Many dishes are creations to showcase Texas products, but others are clearly from both the German and Italian heritage of the owners.

In *Vineyard Cuisine* (Bright Sky Press, 2007), there are recipes for Sicilian meatballs and miniature German rouladen, wine-soaked bratwurst and venison knishes, salmoriglio (a Sicilian sauce) and zwiebelkuchen (a bread with a filling of onion, bacon, eggs, and sour cream). Guests at the Villa are treated to a champagne breakfast that might include a puffy pancake, banana bread with Muscat or southern biscuits, pinot grigio applesauce, a spinach bacon quiche, or eggs Florentine.

When Paul's grandfather came to America, he brought with him his special salad recipe, which has a story behind it. In 1863 Paulo III wished to propose to Antoinette, the "most beautiful woman in all of Sicily," so he invited her family to dinner. But the day of the dinner was the beginning of harvest, and he had no time to gather the food he would need. He raided his garden and created Paulo's salad. The anchovies were to show the depth of his love, symbolically representing the depth of the sea, and the romaine lettuce reflected the freshness of Antoinette's beauty. Of course, he used a family wine in the dressing. ★

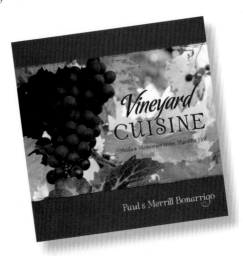

Paulo's Salad
Serves 2

3 anchovies
1 Tbsp. minced garlic
2 Tbsp. Messina Hof Port
2 Tbsp. soy sauce
2 Tbsp. Dijon mustard
2 Tbsp. olive oil
2 Tbsp. balsamic vinegar
2 Tbsp. lemon juice
1 egg
12 whole romaine leaves
¼ cup croutons
2 Tbsp. grated Romano cheese

Combine all ingredients but lettuce and croutons at tableside. Submerge each lettuce leaf in the dressing, shake off the excess, and fan onto salad plates. Top with croutons and cheese. Serve with crostini. It is meant to be finger good.

Here are some other Messina Hof recipes:

Lobster Rockefeller
Serves 2

2 lobster tails in shells, 12 oz. each
4 cups water
1¼ cups Messina Hof Chardonnay
1 cup lemon juice
2 Tbsp. chopped fresh spinach
1 Tbsp. chopped shallots
1¼ cups heavy whipping cream
Salt and pepper to taste
2 Tbsp. hollandaise sauce
2 Tbsp. seasoned breadcrumbs

In large pot, poach lobster tails in water, wine, and lemon juice for about eight minutes. Meanwhile, in a small saucepan, cook spinach and shallots in cream until thickened. Season with salt and pepper. Crack lobster tails to expose all meat. Top with spinach mixture and drizzle with hollandaise. Broil for about two minutes to brown. Finish with breadcrumbs.

Texas Port Tiramisu

    2 cups espresso
    1 bottle Messina Hof Papa Paulo Texas Port
    2½ cups sugar, divided
    9 egg yolks
    ¾ lb. cream cheese, softened
    1 vanilla bean, split lengthwise
    1½ pounds mascarpone cheese
    1 pint heavy whipping cream
    90 ladyfingers, more or less, depending on size
    3 cups shaved semisweet chocolate

In large bowl, combine espresso, wine, and 1 cup sugar. Set aside. In large mixing bowl, whip egg yolks and remaining sugar until light and creamy. Add cream cheese and whip until smooth. Scrape pulp from vanilla bean; add to cream cheese mixture. Fold in mascarpone cheese. Whip cream until stiff peaks form; fold into mascarpone mixture.

    Soak ladyfingers, a few at a time, in espresso mixture. Place in a single layer in 10-inch square pan. Top with a layer of mascarpone mixture and then shaved chocolate. Repeat until pan is filled to the top. Refrigerate two hours before serving.

Dipping Sauce for Bread

    1 Tbsp. dried thyme
    1 Tbsp. paprika
    1 tsp. garlic powder
    1 tsp. onion powder
    1 tsp. salt
    ¼ tsp. black pepper
    Pinch of cayenne (more if you want it more fiery)

Purée in blender until smooth. Put 1 tsp. in small bowl and add olive oil to cover. For an extra zing, add a splash of balsamic vinegar.

    Makes ¼ cup.

Jon Bonnell
Bonnell's Fine Texas Cuisine, Fort Worth

JON BONNELL'S CONTRIBUTION TO TEXAS CUISINE is to bring the fresh products of Texas into the fine dining room. His definition of Texas cuisine is a blend of flavors from our neighboring regional cuisines, combined with ingredients that are uniquely Texan. So Bonnell drives around Fort Worth and Tarrant County collecting local produce; he gets his goat cheese from a farm just down the road from his restaurant, and he welcomes farmers who bring their produce to him. The wild game for which he is increasingly becoming known comes from Texas—quail, venison, feral hogs, fresh seafood. But don't shy away from Bonnell's if you don't want game—the restaurant has a full and varied menu.

Bonnell attended Vanderbilt University, graduating in 1994. After that, he went on to teach science and math in Dallas, but after two years he knew his heart wasn't in teaching. His passion was cooking, and he set out to become a chef. Bonnell enrolled in the New England Culinary Institute where he studied classic methods of preparation. His internship was at Mr. B's Bistro in New Orleans, where he picked up Creole influences for his cooking. But after graduation in 1997, Bonnell headed back to Fort Worth.

He worked as a chef at Randall's Gourmet Cheesecake Factory, a restaurant many Fort Worthians remember both for its rich dessert cheesecakes and its savory non-dessert cheesecakes with salmon, dill, capers, caviar, and whatever goes into a good appetizer. Bonnell left to plan his own restaurant, though he helped open Escargot, a spin-off of the favorite Chardonnay Restaurant. In the fall of 2001, he opened Bonnell's Fine Texas Cuisine. He says one of his assignments at the Culinary Institute was to create a culinary concept and menu for a restaurant. He began by researching farmers and ranchers in the Fort Worth area—and the result was Bonnell's.

The restaurant is not overtly cowboy, as one might suspect from its menu. Instead, it is quiet and sophisticated, with dividers cutting the dining room into small, intimate spaces. Decorative colors are muted, and diners can expect a peaceful, quiet experience lingering over dinner.

The menu offers such delicacies as Bandera Grilled Quail, served with a jalapeño and garlic cream sauce, mashed potatoes, and spicy Parmesan creamed spinach, or Rocky Mountain Elk Tenderloin, accompanied by bacon-laced refried black beans with spicy yellow tomato sauce and micro-greens. The Buffalo Tenderloin is crusted with black pepper, pan seared, and served with a silky whiskey cream sauce. The appetizer menu offers venison carpaccio, elk mini tacos, and oysters Texasfeller. Bonnell says he grew up hunting and eating game, and it's only natural to bring it into his restaurant. The feral pig population in Texas is out of control; Bonnell does his part to control this explosion by serving wild boar chops in the restaurant. He insists that game meat is leaner, has less fat, and is richer in flavor, some of the healthiest meat you can eat. His customers seem delighted.

Bonnell has been honored as a Rising Star of American Cuisine by the James Beard Foundation and a Rising Star by the *Dallas Morning News* after he won the Dallas Food and Wine Festival's Chef competition in 2004. His restaurant has earned awards as Best New Restaurant and Best Southwest Restaurant from *Fort Worth* magazine, and he was named Best Chef by *Fort Worth Weekly* in 2001 and 2004. The Texas Restaurant Association named Bonnell the Outstanding Restaurateur of the Year in 2004. The award that most thrills him is an "excellent" rating in the 2007 Zagat survey of Texas, where Bonnell's was voted one of the Top 10 Restaurants in the

Dallas/Fort Worth Metroplex.

Teaching is a large part of what Jon Bonnell does. Teaching is a part of cooking according to Bonnell. He conducts classes at Central Market, Fort Worth Culinary School, and at Texas Christian University. Nothing in his kitchen is a secret, and he shares his recipes freely. Did you particularly like the Chicken and Wild Mushroom Pasta with Truffles? Go to the website, http://bonnellstexas.com, click on recipes, and ask for it.

Bonnell has now joined the string of restaurants on the "drag" near Texas Christian University. He opened Buffalo Bros. in the fall of 2007, specializing in homemade pizza by the slice, subs, and buffalo wings. There's even a walkup window for students.

Being a chef is fun, according to Jon Bonnell. "Everyone wants to meet the chef, talk to the chef." And he's having the time of his life. ★

Oysters Texasfeller
> 12 Galveston Bay oysters, live (or any other type if those are not available live)
> 1 cup flour
> 2 Tbsp. Creole seasoning
> 1 minced shallot
> 1 clove garlic, minced
> 1 tsp. butter
> 2 cups fresh spinach, chopped
> 1 small bunch cilantro, chopped
> $1/3$ cup diced Tasso ham (or substitute pancetta or salt pork if Tasso is not available)
> 1 splash dry white wine
> Salt and pepper
> Hollandaise sauce

Clean and shuck oysters, removing from shells. Discard top half of shells. Dredge oysters in mixture of flour and Creole seasoning until >>>>>>>>>

11

well coated. Fry in oil heated to 375° for about 2 minutes. Drain oysters on paper towel.

In sauté pan over medium heat cook shallot and garlic in butter. Place Tasso, spinach, and cilantro into pan. Then splash in a bit of white wine and cook until spinach is wilted. Season to taste with salt and pepper. Put the cooked oyster and a small scoop of the spinach mixture back into each shell; top with hollandaise.

Venison Carpaccio with Green Peppercorn Dressing

6 oz. venison backstrap, cleaned of all fat
1 bunch arugula
2 Tbsp. capers
2 caper berries per plate
extra virgin olive oil
1 lemon

Wrap the venison in plastic wrap and freeze solid.

Unwrap, then slice extremely thin on an electric slicer, then cover a chilled plate with one layer of venison.

Cover with plastic wrap until ready to serve. If you do not have a slicer, cut the backstrap into thin pieces, then pound thinner between two layers of plastic (or in a plastic bag).

Fry the capers in vegetable oil until they stop bubbling in the oil and dry on a paper towel.

Dress the arugula greens with olive oil, a squeeze of lemon, and salt, then place a small nest in the center of the plate on top of the venison.

Drizzle the green peppercorn dressing across the plate. Sprinkle the plate with the crisp capers and top with two caper berries. Crack some fresh black pepper over the plate and serve.

Green Peppercorn Dressing

3.5 oz. can of green peppercorns
2 cups mayonnaise
2 cups sour cream
4 lemons, juice only
Zest of 2 lemons, chopped
3 oz. Dijon mustard
1 Tbsp. Worcestershire
Salt and white pepper to taste

Purée the peppercorns with lemon juice in a food processor or blender. Combine with the other ingredients.

Tequila Flamed Quail and Green Chili Cheese Grits

Green Chili Cheese Grits

1 tsp. butter
½ cup chopped onion
1 roasted poblano chili (chopped)

>>>>>>>>>>>

1 tsp. chopped garlic
1 cup chicken stock
1 cup heavy cream
½ cup quick grits
2 oz. grated cheddar cheese
2 oz. grated jack cheese
Salt and pepper to taste
Creole seasoning blend to taste

Sauté the chilies, onions, and garlic in butter until soft.

Add cream and chicken stock and bring to simmer (the stage just before a rolling boil). Be careful not to let the liquids boil over.

Quickly whisk in seasonings and grits. Stir constantly until grits begin to thicken.

Gently fold in cheeses and let sit for at least 5 minutes.

Tequila Flamed Quail
6 oz. cleaned boneless quail meat (diced)
1 oz. gold tequila
salt and pepper to taste
1 shallot (diced)
olive oil
1 poblano pepper (roasted, peeled, and seeded)
queso fresco to garnish
pico de gallo to garnish
1 clove garlic
flour tortilla for serving
1 oz. red pepper (diced)
2 oz. chicken stock
1 serrano chili (diced)

In a hot non-stick skillet brown the quail meat in olive oil, then season with salt and pepper.

Add in the remaining solid ingredients and cook until soft.

Deglaze with chicken stock and reduce by half.

Add tequila and allow to flame (never pour straight from the bottle, pour from a separate glass).

Fill a serving dish with green chili cheese grits and then top with quail, pico de gallo, and queso fresco.

Serve with flour tortilla chips.

★

Randy Evans
Brennan's of Houston
The Kitchen Table: Brennan's of Houston

As EXECUTIVE CHEF, RANDY EVANS PRESIDES over the kitchen at Brennan's of Houston. He's only in his thirties, but he's hitched his career to the Brennan family tradition, giants of Creole cooking. Brennan's came to Houston in 1967, and Randy Evans went to work there as a line cook in 1996. Evans worked his way up through every station and rank in the kitchen. Chef Carl Walker recognized Randy's passion for food and said, "This kid has it!" When Walker became general manager in 2003, Randy became executive chef.

Evans grew up near his grandfather's farm eating fresh produce in season and watching his mother bake country desserts. He planned to become a doctor, like his sister, and spent five semesters at Baylor University majoring in biology. But in his free hours he gave dinner parties and collected antique cookbooks. One day he knew the kitchen was where he belonged. He left Baylor to study at The Art Institute of Houston.

Evans inherited some traditions when he became executive chef, but he has adapted gracefully to them. In the 1990s, Alex Brennan-Martin suggested to Carl Walker that they invite guests into the

15

kitchen. There were possible problems—guests could be in the way, they might get hurt, but Brennan-Martin had grown up in a house where the best part of the party was later in the kitchen, and Walker had been to those parties. They began the Kitchen Table, a table right in the middle of the work area where guests could watch the chefs at work, make eye contact with them, and see their passion for food. In 1997, an expansion of the kitchen led to an enlarged Kitchen Table area, now flanked by a concrete brick wall with hundreds of signatures and messages from happy diners.

Brennan's diners often wandered back into the kitchen, wanting to get involved. This led to Open Kitchen Night. On Wednesdays in June and July, guests can mingle with the team, share cooking conversation, sip some wine or a margarita, and get an inside look at a professional kitchen. The next step was almost inevitable—Chef of the Day. In this program, novices work with the staff and learn to prepare a multi-course meal. Then he or she has dinner in the kitchen with hand-picked guests. What a treat to be able to say, "I helped cook this meal!"

These special programs have continued under Randy Evans' leadership. But under Randy's direction, the cuisine at Brennan's of Houston has become Texas Creole. He is passionate about using local produce, often handpicking produce from a farmer's truck. He talks knowledgeably about the varieties of peas—lady creamers, purple hulls and cream crowders—and what to do with them.

Evans developed a seven-course tasting menu for the Kitchen Table, beginning with a *lagniappe* or "a little something extra"—it may be smoked catfish mousse, shrimp beignets, Creole gravlax, tempura crab-stuffed squash blossoms, or crawfish maque choux. Then comes a soup course, a salad, and charcuterie. Evans became particularly interested in the French art of the charcutier, which means "cooker of meats."

He has traveled throughout Europe studying curing and cooking methods, and his charcuteries course may consist of honey-cured bacon, Tasso ham, wild boar terrine, lamb and rosemary sausage, or foie gras torchon. He often accompanies the charcuteries with his own jellies and jams or pickled vegetables—Meyer lemon marmalade and jelly, mayhaw jelly, prickly pear jelly, white pepper strawberry preserves, peach preserves, pickled green tomatoes, shaved pickled celery. The next course is seafood, then meat, the "forgotten course" of cheese, and dessert.

Of the cheese course, Evans suggests that a cheese platter should consist only of three to five handmade cheeses—at least one cow's milk cheese, one goat's milk, and one sheep's milk. There should be a soft-ripened or triple-cream, a washed-rind cheese, a sharp aged cheddar, and a blue cheese. For a cheese course with dinner, count on three ounces per person; for a cocktail party where it is offered alone, five ounces. Serve it at 65-68° degrees, so remove it from the refrigerator an hour before serving. Accompany with fruits, both dry and fresh, nuts, baguettes, and—his favorite—a honeycomb.

Randy Evans was named King at the Great American Seafood Cook Off, sponsored by the Louisiana Seafood Board, for his Wild Caught Texas Shrimp with Biscuits and Gravy. *Texas Monthly* recognized him as one of three Chefs of the Future, and *My Table* named him Upcoming Chef of the Year. In 2003, he was one of ten national Bertolli Sous Chefs.

Houston Chronicle writer Allison Cook praises Evans for restoring Brennan's former glory. "Brennan's food these days has a profound Southern soulfuness to it. The menu is . . . responsive to the seasons and to the local growers and producers," she wrote. ★

Red Beans and Rice Soup
Serves 10–12

2 Tbsp. vegetable oil
2 cups diced yellow onions
1 cup diced celery
4 cloves garlic, crushed
1 cup diced bell pepper
¼ pound Tasso ham, diced
1 pound dried red beans, rinsed and sorted
6 quarts water
2 Tbsp. Louisiana hot sauce
2 Tbsp. Worcestershire sauce
2 bay leaves
1 sprig fresh thyme
1½ Tbsp. kosher salt
½ tsp. white pepper

Wild Rice Relish
½ Tbsp. vegetable oil
½ cup cooked wild rice
½ cup finely diced tasso ham
1 tsp. minced chives

For the soup:
Heat oil in a large saucepan over medium-high heat; sauté onions, celery, bell pepper, and garlic for 4-5 minutes or until lightly browned. Add ham; cook 2 minutes longer. Add remaining ingredients. Bring to a simmer; cover and cook for 1½ hours or until beans are tender.

Remove from heat; purée with a hand blender until smooth. Adjust consistency with water and adjust seasonings. If desired, strain through a medium mesh strainer.

For the relish:
Heat the oil in a small sauté pan over medium heat; cook rice and ham until heated through.

To plate: Spoon relish in center of warm bowls; ladle hot soup around it, trying not to disturb the rice. Sprinkle with chives.

Halibut Provençal
Serves 4

4 boneless skinless block-cut halibut fillets
(6 oz. each)
Salt and white pepper to taste
3 Tbsp. olive oil, divided
12 spears jumbo asparagus, blanched
1 recipe Yellow and Red Tomato Confit
1 recipe Olive Tapenade
1 recipe Chive Oil

Season fillets with salt and pepper. Heat 2 Tbsp. olive oil in a large sauté pan over medium-high heat; sear halibut, belly side down, for 1 minute. Reduce heat to medium; cook 2 minutes longer. Do not turn over. Finish the halibut in a 450° oven for 4-5 minutes. Remove fillets from pan, flipping over with seared side facing up. Rest for 2 minutes.

For the Yellow and Red Tomato Confit:
4 yellow tomatoes, halved, peeled and seeded
4 Roma tomatoes, halved, peeled and seeded
¼ cup extra virgin olive oil
Kosher salt and cracked black pepper to taste
Red wine vinegar to taste

Toss the yellow and red tomatoes separately with oil, salt, and pepper. Place on a parchment-lined baking sheet. Bake at 250° for 1½ hours or until partially dehydrated. Remove from the pan and refrigerate tomatoes in oil. Mince the tomatoes finely, keeping them separate. In separate small bowls, combine the tomatoes with a touch of vinegar and seasonings. Reserve for garnish. >>>>>>>>>

For the Olive Tapenade:
1 Tbsp. olive oil
1 cup brunoise [method of dicing] yellow onion
½ Tbsp. minced garlic
1 brunoise roasted red bell pepper
1 Tbsp. minced anchovies
1 Tbsp. minced capers
½ cup brunoise black olives, pitted
2 Tbsp. toasted sliced almonds
½ Tbsp. Herbes de Provence
2 Tbsp. red wine vinegar
Salt to taste

Heat oil over medium heat in a small sauté pan; sweat the onion and garlic for 3 minutes. Remove from heat; add bell pepper, anchovies, capers, olives, almonds, and herbs. Stir in the vinegar, ½ Tbsp. at a time, until the desired consistency and flavor are reached. Place in a small container to cool. Adjust seasoning to taste.

For the Chive Oil:
½ cup minced chives
2 cups water
¼ cup salt
½ cup vegetable oil

Place chives in a fine mesh strainer. Bring water and salt to a boil; pour over chives over the sink. Dip strainer into an ice-water bath. Place chives in a blender with half of the oil; purée. Scrape down sides of blender. While processing, slowly add remaining oil. Transfer to a nonreactive container; refrigerate overnight. Strain oil through cheesecloth to remove chive particles. Reserve oil until needed.

To plate: Sauté asparagus in remaining olive oil over medium-high heat for 3 minutes; season with salt and pepper. Arrange asparagus in center of plate with tips pointing out and ends meeting in the middle. Place a tsp. of yellow confit next to asparagus; place ½ Tbsp. of tapenade next to the confit. Place a tsp. of red tomato confit on the other side of the tapenade. Center halibut over asparagus. Dribble chive oil around the plate. Serve immediately.

★

Bill Cauble and Cliff Teinert

Chuck Wagon Cooks, Albany

Barbecue, Biscuits and Beans: Chuck Wagon Cooking

AT FIRST, YOU MIGHT NOT THINK of Bill Cauble and Cliff Teinert as great chefs. They're chuck wagon cooks, cowboys. They use the old methods from the nineteenth century in an authentically restored chuck wagon. You can't go to their restaurant, but you can study their cookbook and follow their recipes around a campfire, in your own backyard, or for an elegant dinner party. The book is *Barbecue, Biscuits and Beans: Chuck Wagon Cooking* (Bright Sky Press, 2002).

In preserving chuck wagon cooking, Cauble and Teinert are aware that they are preserving a vital part of Texas' heritage. Legendary Panhandle rancher Charles Goodnight invented the chuck wagon in the late nineteenth century. Cowboys were driving cattle from Texas to railheads in the North, mostly in Kansas, and they needed three good meals a day on the trail. Goodnight outfitted a wagon with all that's necessary for cooking.

The chuck wagon had to survive rough treatment on the prairies—old army wagons could be converted into usable chuck wagons. The wagon was outfitted with a chuck box, shelves, and drawers. Tin coverings protected goods from rain and, pulled out to make a table, provided a surface for cooks to roll out dough, cut meat, and do other chores. From this wagon, with a Dutch oven, a pot, and a campfire, chuck wagon cooks could provide fried beef, beans, biscuits, and coffee on the trail for hungry cowboys. It's part of our image of the American West.

Bill Cauble claims his mother made him learn to cook as a child. A native of Albany, Texas, he worked in the oil fields of

West Texas and had a very successful career as an artist, (he is still an artist, drawing and painting in bits of spare time) but then he came home to Albany and became a cook and a manager for friend and mentor Watt Matthews of the Lambshead Ranch. He cooked breakfast for the cowboys and the Matthews family, owners of the ranch, and lunch and dinner for an assemblage of family, friends, any visitors, sometimes as many as thirty or forty people . . . and of course the marvelous parties, planned or spontaneous: simple, plain, or elegant. What did Cauble learn? Cowboys like meat, beans, potatoes, bread, and corn. They'll eat green vegetables if they're fried. And they want ranch dressing on everything. It all made cooking a real challenge. He sets up his authentic restored chuck wagon on the courthouse lawn and cooks his fabulous barbecue brisket suppers for the town and visitors before Fandangle performances each June.

Cliff Teinert grew up in Central Texas, with grandparents born in Germany. Staples in his family's household were homemade egg noodles, sausage, and fresh beef. As a young man, he moved to Albany to work on a relative's ranch, but by 1970 he was in the catering business. Watt Matthews of Lambshead gave him the shell of an old chuck wagon, and he rebuilt it. He cooked for the annual Fandangle outdoor play staged in Albany and in Johnson City. Those dining on his food included presidents Lyndon Johnson, Ronald Reagan, George H. W. Bush, and former Mexican President Juan Lopez Portillo. His menu grew beyond the usual chuck wagon fare to include fish, New Mexican influences, breads, and desserts.

Cauble and Teinert helped found the Western Chuck Wagon Association, which now sponsors annual competitions. One allows wood-burning stoves and the things you'd find in a camp that moved only occasionally; the other disallows anything that could not be carried on a long journey and moved daily.

Don't be mistaken: Chuck wagon cooking can provide elegant fare. One of the team's favorite dinners is a whole rib eye cooked over mesquite coals with grilled vegetables, ranch rolls, and bread pudding.

Cauble and Teinert insist on cast iron for cooking. It conducts heat well and cleans easily if properly cared for. A properly cured Dutch oven is a prize today. Using a well-cured Dutch oven, this team of cooks may prepare eggplant, German potato salad, butternut squash soup, venison, rack of lamb or crown roast, stacked red chile enchiladas, game hens, dove, and wild turkey. Off the grill they prepare salads such as cornbread salad and a superior slaw. Chuck wagon cooking today is not what it was in the heyday of the trail drives and the cowboy.

These chefs prepare a breakfast as wonderful as the dinners they cook. ★

Tissa's Dutch Oven Breakfast
   Serves 4–6

   2 Tbsp. extra virgin olive oil
   1 cup chopped onion
   ½ sweet red pepper, chopped
   6 oz. chicken breast, cut into bite-sized pieces
   8 oz. spicy pork sausage, cut into bite-sized pieces
   1–2 Tbsp. fresh rosemary, chopped
   2 Tbsp. dry red wine
   10 large eggs
   1½ cups cooked rice
   1 tsp. salt
   ½ tsp. freshly ground black pepper
   ½ cup finely chopped fresh basil
   Preheat oven to 375°.

Heat a 14-inch Dutch oven or large oven-proof skillet over medium heat and add oil. Sauté onion, red pepper, chicken, and sausage until vegetables are soft and meat is thoroughly cooked, about 10 minutes. Stir in rosemary and wine. Sauté for two minutes.

   Turn heat to high. Whisk together eggs, rice, salt, pepper, and basil. When oil begins to smoke, pour egg mixture into Dutch oven on top of vegetables and meat mixture. Remove Dutch oven from heat, stir slightly to mix ingredients completely. Bake 45 minutes or until center is firm. Cook at least 15 minutes.

   Invert onto platter or cut into serving wedges to serve.

Sourdough Starter

   1 2-oz. cake yeast or 3 ¼-oz. packets of dry yeast
   4 cups warm water
   2 Tbsp. sugar
   4 cups all-purpose flour
   1 raw potato, peeled and quartered

Dissolve yeast in warm water. Add sugar, flour, and potato. Mix in crock and let rise until very light and slightly aged. To remix starter, add 1 cup warm water, 2 tsp. sugar, and the amount of flour to mix to consistency of first starter. Set aside until biscuit time again. Never add yeast after the first time, but keep raw potato in as food for the starter. For best results, use daily. Store in refrigerator.

Sourdough Biscuits

   4 cups sourdough starter
   4 cups all-purpose flour, sifted
   1 tsp. salt
   2 Tbsp. sugar
   3 heaping tsp. baking power
   4 Tbsp. shortening
   Preheat oven to 350°.

Put flour in large bowl and form a hollow. Pour starter into the hollow. Add sugar, salt, baking powder, and shortening. Mix well to form soft dough.

   Pinch off bits of dough the size of an egg and place in well-greased 14-inch Dutch bread oven or skillet. Grease tops of biscuits generously and set them in a warm place to rise for 5 to 10 minutes before baking.

   Bake for 30 minutes or until nicely browned. The closer the biscuits are crowded into the pan, the higher they will rise.

   When cooking in a covered Dutch oven over coals, consistent heat for baking is important. Beware of wind and drafts, which can result in uneven heat. Yields 30 biscuits.

Brisket

The best brisket is cooked over coals, not flame. Cauble and Teinert prefer mesquite wood for their coals. For mopping they use a clean wash cloth or rag, with no strings to hang down. They tie a wire around the cloth to move mopping sauce to meat, but they say you might use a long-handled brush.

1 brisket, seven to eleven pounds

Coat with brisket rub and cook 12-13 hours until internal temperature is 180°. Mop with mopping sauce each time the brisket is turned; keep the mopping sauce warm. Do not mop during the last two hours of cooking. Serves 8-10.

Brisket Rub

2 Tbsp. freshly ground black pepper
1 Tbsp. kosher salt or sea salt
1 tsp. garlic powder
1 tsp. onion powder
1 tsp. dried parsley
1 Tbsp. chili powder
1 tsp. oregano
1 tsp. sugar

Mix all ingredients and rub on brisket. May be stored in dry container two to three weeks.

Mopping Sauce

1 cup apple cider vinegar
1 cup vegetable oil
1 cup red wine, Burgundy or Chianti
2 cups water
2 sliced lemons
1 sliced onion
2 cloves garlic
1 Tbsp. chili powder
1 Tbsp. freshly ground black pepper
1 tsp. kosher salt or sea salt

Bring all ingredients to boil. Remove from heat and use to mop the brisket.

Helen Corbitt
The Zodiac Room, Neiman Marcus, Dallas
The Best from Helen Corbitt's Kitchen

NO BOOK OF TEXAS CHEFS WOULD BE COMPLETE WITHOUT the late and legendary Helen Corbitt, the woman Stanley Marcus called the "Balenciaga of Food." In a state known for barbecue, beans, and Tex-Mex, she created lobster thermidor and strawberries Romanoff. She wasn't to Texas cooking what Julia Child was to French cooking, because she brought French cooking to us rather than adapting to Texas.

In truth, Helen Corbitt, an easterner by birth, hated Texas—at least at first. When she moved to Houston, it took her six months to unpack her suitcase and a year to unpack her trunk—she kept thinking she could move back east. Asked to prepare a meal with Texas ingredients, she invented Texas caviar, that spicy dish based on black-eyed peas. Now we see it everywhere in all kinds of versions. Corbitt's version is simple and straightforward. Eventually, she called herself a "Texan by adoption."

Nor did she mean to be a chef. Born in 1906 in upstate New York, she attended Skidmore College. She wanted to become a doctor, but she got a degree in home economics. When her family lost everything in the Depression, she put that degree to work by serving as a therapeutic dietitian in hospitals. The work held no charm for her, and she was looking for a new position when the University of Texas at Austin offered her a position teaching quantity cooking classes and tea room management.

From the university, she moved to Houston and created a reputation for sensational food at the Houston Country Club. That proved to be more responsibility than she wanted, and

27

she went next to run the restaurants in the downtown Joske's Department Store. Corbitt insisted on the freshest fruits and vegetables, and she wanted the latter cooked al dente—no soggy, overcooked broccoli. Typical of her day, she made lots of molded salads, and she used butter and sour cream with abandon, though she usually recommended half and half instead of pure cream. She dispensed such tidbits as the fact that an odd number of shrimp on a plate looks better than an even number.

Although she was told she would have complete control at Joske's, she soon found that management did not appreciate her insistence on only the finest ingredients. Next she went to the Driskill Hotel in Austin, where she became friends with Lyndon Johnson and his family. LBJ wanted her to come to the White House, but she refused. Perhaps she was getting used to Texas.

Stanley Marcus had wanted her to take over the Zodiac Room in the downtown Dallas Neiman Marcus store almost ever since she came to Texas, but she kept taking new jobs elsewhere in the state. Marcus was persistent, and in 1955 she moved to Dallas. It was the job that would be called the highpoint of her career. When people said Marcus made her reputation, she protested that she had her reputation before her years at the Zodiac Room.

Helen Corbitt was a red-headed Irish woman with a temper to match. She had a sharp sense of humor and a strong personality. Independent, sassy, impatient, and a perfectionist, she brooked no interference. Even Stanley Marcus was not allowed in her kitchen without invitation. But throughout her life she developed a cadre of loyal friends and employees, because she cared about people.

She presided over the Neiman's restaurant until 1969 when she retired to travel and lecture. During those years

she also taught cooking classes in her home, the most famous being the "No Name Gourmet School for Men." She wrote several cookbooks: *Helen Corbitt's Cookbook, Helen Corbitt's Potluck, Helen Corbitt Cooks for Looks, Helen Corbitt Cooks for Company,* and *Helen Corbitt's Greenhouse Cookbook.* She had by 1978 become interested in developing low-calorie menus for the Neiman Marcus spa, The Greenhouse. In the late 1960s, told that she must lose weight, she developed her own diet, according to the principles learned in her hospital dietitian days, and lost a dramatic amount of weight. In 2000, the University of North Texas Press published *The Best from Helen Corbitt's Kitchens,* edited by Patty Vineyard MacDonald.

Corbitt's many awards include the gold Escoffier plaque from the Confrérie de la Chaîne des Rôtisseurs, the world's oldest gourmet society, and the Golden Plate Award from the Institutional Food Service Manufacturers' Association. Skidmore College awarded her an honorary Ph.D. and the University of Dallas presented its Athena Award for her indomitable spirit and impeccable character. ★

Pickled Black-Eyed Peas
2 15-oz. cans cooked dried black-eyed peas
1 cup salad oil
¼ cup wine vinegar
1 whole clove garlic—or garlic seasoning
¼ cup thinly sliced onion
½ tsp. salt
Cracked or freshly ground black pepper

Drain peas. Mix all ingredients and store in jar in refrigerator. Remove garlic after one day. Store at least two days and up to two weeks before eating.

Lobster Thermidor
Serves 2

1 2-lb. lobster
4 Tbsp. butter, divided
2 Tbsp. flour
1 cup cream or milk or half-and-half
¼ tsp. salt
½ tsp. dry mustard
4 Tbsp. sherry
1 egg yolk
1 cup fresh mushrooms, quartered
½ cup Parmesan cheese, grated
Paprika

Boil the lobster and split lengthwise. Remove all the meat and cut into one-inch cubes. [Preheat the oven to 375°.] Melt 2 Tbsp. of the butter in a skillet, add flour and cook until bubbly, then gradually add cream, salt, and mustard; cook until thick; add the

sherry and egg yolk, stirring thoroughly. Keep warm over hot water. Sauté mushrooms in remaining 2 Tbsp. of butter and add the lobster meat. Swish around, then add the sherry sauce to it. Sprinkle part of the cheese in the bottom of the lobster shells, add the mixture and sprinkle remaining cheese on top. Sprinkle with a little paprika and brown in the oven. You could do these ahead of time and freeze them, then brown when ready to serve.

Strawberries Romanoff

Serves 6

1 pint vanilla ice cream
1 cup heavy cream
½ cup plus 1 Tbsp. Cointreau, divided
1 quart fresh strawberries
½ cup confectioners' sugar

Whip ice cream until it is creamy and fold in whipped cream and 6 Tbsp. of Cointreau. Fold in strawberries, sweetened with sugar and add 3 Tbsp. of Cointreau. Blend quickly and lightly and serve in chilled, stemmed glasses. The hostess should do this at the table.

★

The Best from
Helen Corbitt's
Kitchens

EDITED BY PATTY VINEYARD MACDONALD

Dean Fearing

Fearing's, Dallas

The Mansion on Turtle Creek Cookbook and
Dean Fearing's Southwest Cuisine: Blending Asia & the Americas

FOR TWENTY-ONE YEARS THE NAMES DEAN FEARING and The Mansion on Turtle Creek were inseparable. As executive chef, Fearing made The Mansion one of Texas' most outstanding restaurants, earning a Mobil Five-Star rating. His creative dishes began with seasonal native foods—Texas-grown chile peppers, jicama, cilantro, tomatillos, and avocado; he cooked wild game and birds from the Hill Country. An international traveler, he incorporated influences of Italian, Thai, southern, Cajun, and Mexican cuisines into his cooking. He created such dishes as Carne Asado of Ostrich Filet and Papaya Molé Glazed Quail with Smoked Corn Enchiladas. And he earned countless awards, including the 1994 James Beard Perrier-Jouet Restaurant Award as Best Chef and a turn on the cover of *Gourmet* magazine. He made The Mansion famous—and it made him famous.

Fearing was born in Louisville, Kentucky, and his southern roots have stayed with him. He studied at the Culinary Institute of America and then began his career at Maisonette in Cincinnati. In 1979 he came to Dallas and the Pyramid Room at the Fairmount Hotel. In 1980, he joined the staff at the new Mansion on Turtle Creek as executive sous chef, and in 1985 became executive chef. After a brief stay at Agnews, a restaurant featuring Southwestern cuisine, he was back at The Mansion. He described it as a homecoming.

Early in 2007, Fearing announced that he would leave The Mansion to become chef and partner in the then unnamed restaurant in the Ritz-Carlton planned for Uptown in Dallas.

The restaurant, now named Fearing's, opened in August 2007 to much fanfare. It was the opportunity he couldn't turn down—a chance to have his own venture and to be a partner.

Fearing's offers seven dining and gathering settings and is noted for Texas farm-to-market specialties. One of his most popular dinner dishes is Maple Black Peppercorn Soaked Buffalo Tenderloin on Anson Mills Jalapeño Grits, accompanied by a Crispy Butternut Squash Taquito. Want an appetizer? How about Barbecued Bluepoint Oysters with Artichokes, Spinach, and Gulf Crab Meat? Brunch offerings include Jaxson & Campbell-style Pancake—all you can eat—with Guernsey Butter, Vermont Maple Syrup, and Apple Smoked Bacon, or Texas Pecan-Fried Quail in Cream, and Sweet Potato Spoon Bread with Blue Cheese Slaw.

Fearing has added an innovative Afternoon Tea to the menu, with dishes such as skewered Norwegian Smoked Salmon, Dill Cream Cheese and Caviar on Pumpernickel, Watercress, Sliced Egg, and Watercress on Whole Wheat, and other unusual finger sandwich selections. There is also a Light Tea, a Royal Tea, and a Children's Tea—PBJ finger sandwiches, ham & American Cheese with Mayonnaise finger sandwiches, chocolate-dipped strawberries, and other delicacies.

An exuberant personality, Fearing wears colorful Lucchese boots with his chef's whites. He plays "progressive Texas country" on a classic Fender guitar with a group of musical chefs known as The Barbwires. Fascinated by barbecue, he and his friends sponsor an annual fundraiser barbecue for the Texas Scottish Rite Hospital for Children. He hosts two television shows—"Dean's Cuisine" and "A Taste of the Southwest" and is the author of cookbooks: *The Mansion on Turtle Creek Cookbook* and *Dean Fearing's Southwest Cuisine: Blending Asia and the Americas.* ★

Tortilla Soup
    Serves 4

    3 Tbsp. corn oil
    4 corn tortillas, cut into long strips
    8 garlic cloves, peeled
    2 cups fresh onion purée
    4 cups fresh tomato purée
    5 dried ancho chiles, fire roasted and seeded (See Note #1)
    2 jalapeños, chopped
    1 Tbsp. cumin powder
    1 Tbsp. epazote, chopped (or 2 Tbsp. chopped fresh cilantro)
    1 tsp. ground coriander
    1 large bay leaf
    1½ quarts chicken stock
    Salt to taste
    Lemon juice to taste
    Cayenne pepper to taste

    For garnish:
    1 smoked chicken breast, skinless, boneless, and diced small
    1 large avocado, peeled, seeded, and cut into small cubes
    ½ cup shredded Boyaca (Latin Cheddar) cheese
    4 Tbsp. green cabbage, small dice
    3 Tbsp. red radish, small dice
    1 Tbsp. jalapeño pepper, seeded and minced
    4 corn tortillas, cut into thin strips and fried crisp

Heat oil in a large saucepan over medium heat. Add tortillas
and garlic and sauté until tortillas are crisp and garlic is golden
brown, about 4 to 5 minutes. Add onion purée and cook for 5
minutes, stirring occasionally until reduced by half. Add tomato
purée, roasted chiles, jalapeños, cumin, coriander, epazote, bay
leaf and chicken stock. Bring to a boil. Lower heat and simmer
for approximately 40 minutes. Skim fat from surface, if necessary.
Process through a food mill to attain the perfect consistency or use
a blender (soup may become thick; thin out with additional chicken
stock). Season to taste with salt, lemon and cayenne

NOTE #1. Using a pair of kitchen tongs, hold each chile directly
over open flame. Lightly roast each chile on all sides for about 30
to 45 seconds. (Be careful not to blacken or burn chiles.) When

chiles are cool, remove seeds and stem. This same process can be done in a preheated 400° oven. Cook chiles for about 2 to 3 minutes.

Garnish each warm soup bowl with smoked chicken breast, avocado, shredded Boyaca cheese, green cabbage, red radish, jalapeño pepper, and corn tortillas. Ladle 8 oz. of tortilla soup over the garnish. Serve immediately.

Maple Black Peppercorn Buffalo Tenderloin

    Six buffalo filets
    Salt to taste
    2 Tbsp. vegetable oil
    1 cup maple syrup
    2 Tbsp. fresh cracked black pepper
    2 cloves garlic, peeled and finely chopped
    1 large shallot, peeled and finely chopped
    1 tsp. finely chopped fresh sage
    1 tsp. finely chopped fresh thyme
    Crushed red pepper flakes to taste

Make glaze first. In a small bowl, combine maple syrup, black pepper, garlic, shallot, sage, thyme and pepper flakes. Stir to combine and set aside.

Season each filet with salt. Heat oil in large cast-iron skillet over medium-high heat. When hot, lay beef filets in skillet and brown for 5 minutes. Turn and brown for an additional 3-5 minutes or until desired degree of doneness is reached.

Just before removing meat, add maple syrup mixture to the skillet to deglaze the pan as well as to glaze the filets. Quickly turn meat over to glaze other side. Remove from skillet immediately.

Lanny Lancarte
Lanny's Alta Cocina, Fort Worth

LANNY LANCARTE II GREW UP IN A MEXICAN restaurant. He's the grandson of Joe T. Garcia, who with his wife, Mama Sus, founded the legendary Joe T. Garcia's that now sprawls across almost an entire city block in North Fort Worth. The famous and the unknown flock to Joe T.'s for the traditional dinner—nachos, cheese enchiladas, tacos, beans, rice, guacamole, and tortillas. In fact, in the evening, fajitas are the only other thing on the menu—and that's a recent addition within the last twenty years or so.

Lanny remembers spending a lot of time in the kitchen, because if he wanted to see his parents, that's where they were. By the time he was eight, he was waiting on a few tables. He studied Spanish and food management in college and then sort of drifted into management at the family business. But he knew he wanted to expand his boundaries. In his early twenties, he went to Oaxaca to study with Diana Kennedy, the legendary chef of Mexico. She had a profound impact on his cooking. What impressed Lancarte the most was her passion for every single ingredient in a dish—every last tomato and chile. "She made me understand that if you don't have respect for the food, it won't come out the way it should," he said.

Lancarte felt the need for classical training, and he enrolled in the Culinary Institute of America in New York. For six months he interned in restaurants owned by Rick Bayless. All reports are that Lanny knew traditional Tex-Mex cooking but was wide open to new suggestions and approaches. When he returned to Fort Worth, Lanny told his father that he enjoyed restaurant management—but his heart was in the kitchen. He wanted to do his own kind of food, and he needed his own kitchen.

His dad built a small kitchen and private dining room buried within the Joe T. Garcia's restaurant complex, just off the patio which takes up fully half the seating space. Lanny filled the shelves with contemporary plates and the pantry and cooler with things Joe T.'s had never housed—duck confit, huitlacoche, pepitas, pistachios, panko, epazote. He began to offer chef's dinners. Customers flocked to the small private room with its feeling of exclusivity.

Lanny trained his staff so that they knew the food as well as he did, and they knew how to serve, from flatware selections to serving from the left and taking from the right. The emphasis was on tasting menus—yes, seven courses but small bites of each, the *amuse bouche* concept that has become so fashionable. And each course served on a different style plate—square, oblong, round, whatever suited the dish being served at the moment. For Lancarte, dining was about the whole experience. Guests realized they were tasting things they had never tasted before.

Lancarte's family knew he wanted to open his own restaurant. The tasting-menu dinners he did at Joe T.'s were all about menu testing. In the summer of 2005 Lancarte, just barely thirty, left the family restaurant and opened his own bistro-like small restaurant in Fort Worth's Cultural District. With sixty seats, Lanny's Alta Cocina is both intimate and independent. It's casual and informal but it works splendidly.

The kitchen crew works in an assembly-line fashion, but Lanny Lancarte touches every plate that leaves his kitchen. He may arrange a crumb or a fresh flower or herb accent. The plate has to be perfect before it is served. He's still waking up palates with new tastes—huitlacoche tamales with rustic corn sauce, a salad with house-cured duck prosciutto, a foie gras French toast with blueberry and hibiscus marmalade, date-crusted prime strip with serrano-wrapped asparagus and roasted fingerlings.

Lanny's Alta Cocina still offers a five-course tasting menu, wine pairings extra, and for a small additional charge—a supplemental foie gras course! And then of course there's dessert—churros with warm cajeta, raspberry goat cheese cake with praline sauce, warm chocolate cake with Kahlua crème Anglaise sauce.

Asked about the future, Lanny said he's pretty settled in learning to run Alta Cocina, which is now two and a half years old. He doesn't want to jump into something else new, but he has ideas for the future … something near the current restaurant but with a banquet facility where he could serve large private parties.

And then there's that cookbook he's been working on for two years. He thinks he had writer's block, but he'll get back to it. He's got the title: *Alta Cocina,* of course. ★

Arctic Char with Jalapeño Beurre Blanc with Spinach Tortilla
Serves 4

4 Arctic Char filets
1 pound flat leaf spinach
8 oz. crème fraîche
7 egg yolks
1 cup white wine
6 peppercorns
1 shallot, sliced
3 cloves garlic, sliced
12 oz. butter
2 jalapeño peppers, minced
1 tomato, finely diced
1 Tbsp. parsley, minced
1 oz. lime juice

For the Tortilla:
Wilt spinach in oil and set aside to cool. Mix egg yolks and crème fraîche together and fold in spinach. Place in non-stick tart molds and cook in 350° oven for 10-12 minutes.

For Buerre Blanc:
Stir shallots, garlic, peppercorns in a tsp. of butter in saucepan over medium heat until translucent. Add white wine and reduce to almost au sec (very little liquid remaining).
Turn down heat and whisk in butter slowly. When all the butter has melted, strain then add jalapeño, tomato, parsley, and lime juice. Season with salt.

Season char with salt and pepper. In sauté pan over medium-high heat sear presentation side first, flip fish, and lower heat until fish is cooked.

Place tortilla on plate, top with char, and spoon beurre blanc around the plate.

Note: Arctic char looks like salmon and tastes like trout. If you cannot get the fish, you can substitute salmon or trout. Char is found in arctic or subarctic waters and glacial lakes. It has a vibrant color and a hearty flesh without oily flavor.

Tim Love
Lonesome Dove and Love Shack, Fort Worth
Tim Love on the Lonesome Dove Trail:
Recipes of Urban Western Cuisine

IT'S AN ILL WIND THAT BLOWS NO GOOD. On March 28, 2000, about 6:25 P.M., an F2 tornado blew through downtown Fort Worth, heavily damaging the Bank One Tower with the Reata restaurant perched on its thirty-fifth floor, among other buildings. Chef Tim Love was working at Reata managing both the front and the back, and the wind that cost him his job blew him into a career as a restaurant entrepreneur. Within three months, he had opened Lonesome Dove, an atmospheric restaurant in the city's fabled Stockyards National Historic District that features "urban western cuisine." The chef wears a cowboy hat instead of a toque.

What's on the menu at his signature restaurant? The basics are steak and wild game—buffalo, antelope, red deer, wild boar. But he varies the dishes with lingonberries from Sweden, Spanish Manchego cheese, or quandong sauce from Australia.

Love went on to buy the legendary White Elephant Saloon, around the corner from his restaurant. The White Elephant has a long tradition behind it. Once the site of a famous shootout between Longhair Jim Courtright and Luke Short, the watering hole attracts both tourists and locals and is noted for its continuous bill of live music, often featuring the best of country singers. Today, a re-enactment of the shootout is staged every year on the anniversary, February 8. Love says the owners, a conglomerate, approached him when they were ready to sell because they wanted someone who would carry on the tradition. He does.

Love next opened Lonesome Dove New York City, which closed after six months, although it got some good reviews. Undaunted he turned his attention back to Fort Worth and opened Duce, a place that served what he called "modern Euro cuisine" but was in reality almost a tapas temple. It offered large and small food, the small being one-bite tapas—but oh so good! The single sea scallop on cauliflower purée and topped with foie gras was a wonder. In 2008, Love sold the restaurant to a Chicago chef.

But in 2007 he had opened the Love Shack, a mostly-outdoor hamburger shack next to the White Elephant, serving what many claim are the best hamburgers in town, along with hand-cut French fries, sausage, and onion rings. And, ever the entrepreneur, in 2008, he announced an affiliation with Z Market, the chain that supplies fresh hot and cold fare to travelers in airports. Z Markets have been described as "upscale convenience stores." Love will provide specially crafted to-go selections for travelers to grab and eat on the plane at the market in Terminal B of the DFW Airport. He will be in good company: legendary chef Wolfgang Puck once provided sandwiches for Z Market.

Love is not a chef, entrepreneur, or westerner by birth or upbringing. Born in Denton, Texas, he is completely self-taught. He was studying at the University of Tennessee in Knoxville for a BA in finance and marketing, when he began working in a kitchen to help put himself through school. He ended up running the kitchen at Kiva, an upscale southwestern restaurant. After school, he went to the Uptown Bistro in Frisco, Colorado, where he won the Taste of Breckenridge Grand Award three years and the Taste of the Mountains Award several times. From there, he came back to Texas to work as executive chef at Mira Vista Country Club and then on to Reata.

Many honors have come to Love. In 2003, he was chosen to cook at the James Beard House for a dinner in honor of Beard's 100th birthday. Love turned the trip into a trail drive, from Fort Worth to New York City. On the ride, he stopped at farmers' markets and bought produce, all of which he used for several dinners along the way. Proceeds went to Spoons Across America, an organization supported by the James Beard Foundation to educate children in culinary matters. The trail drive was covered by the TODAY show, taking it to some 30 million viewers. His second trail drive, in 2004, took him to

Los Angeles for the American Express Celebrity Chef Tour and was made into a TV documentary, "Cowboys on the Trail." Love has appeared, victoriously, on the *Iron Chef* show where he won a chile battle, on *Challenge: Hawaiian Luau Beach BBQ*—a show that brought him national fame on top of his local renown. He's also been on the *Paula Deen Show*, and in such publications as *Bon Appetit, Food & Wine,* and *The Wall Street Journal.*

What's next for the imaginative, ambitious chef? He admits he's looking at two places in Dallas. ★

Some of Tim Love's creations:

Shiner Bock Battered Soft Shell Crawfish with Cilantro Orange Butter Sauce

> 1 quart soft shell crawfish (found in specialty markets only), heads removed
> 4 eggs
> 1 12-oz. Shiner Bock beer
> 2 cups flour
> 1 Tbsp. chile powder
> 1 Tbsp. garlic powder
> 1 Tbsp. salt
> 1 Tbsp. pepper
> 1 quart peanut oil
> 1 Tbsp. shallots, minced
> 1 cup orange juice
> 1 cup white wine
> ¼ cup cilantro, chopped
> ½ pound butter, unsalted
> ¼ cup heavy whipping cream

To prepare Crawfish:
In bowl mix flour, chile powder, garlic powder, salt and pepper. In a separate bowl, mix eggs and beer. Heat peanut oil in a small saucepan to 350°. Put crawfish in flour mixture first, then egg mixture, then back into flour mixture, and straight into the hot oil. Cook for approximately 3 minutes.

>>>>>>>>>➤

To prepare sauce:
In a saucepan add shallots, orange juice, and white wine and bring to a boil. Continue to boil until liquid is almost gone. Add heavy cream and reduce heat to very low. Cut the cold butter into small cubes. Using a whisk, quickly whip in the butter over low heat. Never stop whipping or the sauce will separate. Once all butter is incorporated, add cilantro, salt and pepper to taste.

Serve the sauce in a ceramic dish surrounded by the crawfish and garnish with orange zest.

Roasted Garlic-Stuffed Beef Tenderloin with Western Plaid Hash and Syrah Demi-glâce
Serves 4

1 cup Australian syrah
2 cups veal stock, reduced by half
4 beef tenderloin filets
10 whole cloves garlic, roasted
½ gallon peanut oil
2 russet potatoes
½ cup olive oil
1 cup julienned red pepper
¼ cup minced jalapeño
1 cup julienned red cabbage
1 cup julienned green cabbage
1 cup julienned red onion
Kosher salt and cracked fresh pepper

Place ½ cup wine in a sauce pot and bring to a boil. After half has evaporated, add veal stock and simmer until ready to use. With a paring knife, make a small slit in the side of each tenderloin and stuff 1 large garlic clove in each. Set aside. Place peanut oil in a 4-quart pot and heat to 325°. On a mandoline or by hand, julienne the potatoes to ¼-inch strips and place in cool water to remove some starch. When oil reaches 325°, carefully drop potatoes in oil, stirring frequently. Cook for approximately 4 minutes or until golden brown.

Remove potatoes from oil into a bowl and season with salt and pepper. In a large, hot iron skillet or flat grill, put ¼ cup olive oil. Add peppers, cabbage, onions, and remainder of garlic. Cook until cabbage is wilted, adding salt and pepper to taste. Add remainder of wine to cabbage mixture and simmer. To a hot sauté pan, add ¼ cup olive oil. Season filets by rubbing salt and pepper into the top and bottom of each steak.

Place all four steaks in the pan at once and sear on high for 1½ minutes each side and place in a 350° oven for 4 minutes for medium-rare to medium.

To plate: Place potatoes in center of plate and place the cabbage on top. Place tenderloin on top of the cabbage and pour veal sauce on top of the steak.

Garnish with a seasonal green vegetable like grilled asparagus or green beans.

Ancho Chocolate Cake

¼ cup orange juice
1 cup sugar
6 oz. butter
2 cups chocolate chips
3 dried ancho chiles
4 large eggs
2 tsp. flour
Pinch of salt

Roast chiles in sauté pan 1-2 minutes. Rehydrate chiles with simple syrup. Peel and seed chiles to make purée. Combine juice and sugar and bring to a boil; pour over chocolate. Add butter and chile purée. Add eggs one at a time. Add flour and salt. Pour batter into baking container and place in a bain marie (water bath). Bake at 350° for 45 minutes.

★

Chad Martin
Hôtel St. Germain, Dallas

THE POLAR OPPOSITE OF CHUCK WAGON COOKING, southwestern cuisine and urban western cuisine is the European-style dining opportunity offered at Dallas' Hôtel St. Germain. The hotel, in a renovated Victorian home on Maple Avenue, offers seven luxury suites, parlors, two dining rooms, and a courtyard and is furnished with the owner's personal collection of antiques. But it is the restaurant that draws upscale diners and guests from Dallas and all over.

Dinner is served at two seatings, Tuesday through Saturday. The prix fixe menu is $85 and changes weekly. Reservations are required, and when you make your reservation you must choose your entrée. Gentlemen best not show up without jacket and tie.

But the dining experience is well worth all those requirements. In the dining rooms, tables are set far apart for intimacy, and lighting is so muted that small flashlights are provided for reading the menu. Diners are served on antique Limoges china accompanied by antique silverware, Frette linen, and cut crystal. Dinner plates are covered with silver domes on the trip from the kitchen to table.

What is served? The menu begins with an *amuse bouche* (a bit to please the mouth)—perhaps chickpea salad with feta, a small potato/onion latke with smoked salmon, or escargot in a puff pastry—followed by soup, appetizer, seafood, entrée, fromage or cheese course, dessert, and *mignardise* (a funny little sweet bite to end the meal)—often a praline, with a bow to the owner's New Orleans background, but sometimes a truffle, a pistachio cake, a petit four or perhaps a chocolate-dipped strawberry.

Presiding over this quiet elegance is Chef Chad Martin, a native of Dallas and son of an artist father and a gourmand mother. He was, he says, eating artichokes at the age of four, when other kids had never heard of them. "I was around good

food all the time," he explains. He tried going into art with his father but found everything was headed toward computers. "I like to work with my hands, and cooking calls on my artistic side and also lets me work with my hands." (His creations are as beautiful to behold as they are palate-pleasing.) His mother suggested that, since he liked to cook, he consider culinary school—and off he went to El Centro College, where he met a lot of creative people and made friends in the food business.

It may have been the friends who helped him or it may have been just his own evident talent, but he landed a dream job for a beginning chef—at the Adolphus Hotel. He was there three years and then moved to New York City, a period he considers a learning experience. Working fourteen or fifteen hours six days a week, he perfected his techniques in French cuisine at Café Boulud. Next, a friend told him about an opening at an upscale country club on Cape Cod. "The pay was good, the hours were easier … and it was Cape Cod." He was there two years.

Family and friends lured him back to Dallas where he joined the staff of the Hôtel St. Germain as sous chef in 2000 and accepted the position of chef in 2001. His signature dish? Oysters Rockefeller, which he explains they serve because the hotel owner is from New Orleans. Other specialties include Beef Tenderloin with Foie Gras, Escargot with White Truffles, Sea Bass on Lemon Risotto, and Chocolate Soup with Pistachio Nougat.

Chef Martin's menu is noticeably short of the chiles and peppers that dot so many upscale Texas menus. "We stay away from spice," he said. With a fixed menu, customers don't have a lot of choices, and he keeps that in mind in creating his weekly menu. He draws his inspiration from his family, and when he creates a new dish, he thinks of his mother and her palate. "Her palate is mine, too." ★

Hôtel St. Germain's Oysters Rockefeller

1 dozen shucked oysters, in shell
12 cups spinach, roughly chopped, sautéed and drained of
liquid (reserve liquid)
1 strip smoked bacon, small dice (freeze the bacon
before dicing)
3 shallots, minced
3 garlic cloves, minced
½ celery rib, small dice
¼ cup Pernod liqueur or white wine
1½ cups heavy whipping cream
⅓ cup grated Parmigiano Reggiano
½ cup breadcrumbs
Tabasco or other hot sauce
1 tsp. Worcestershire
Salt and pepper

Sauté the bacon until brown then add the shallot, garlic, and celery
and cook until translucent.

Remove the pan from heat and add the Pernod until it
reduces and return pan to heat. Add the reserved spinach and
the cream and cook above medium heat until mixture is reduced
by half. Stir in Parmigiano Reggiano, breadcrumbs, Tabasco, and
Worcestershire. Season with salt and pepper.

Heat oven to 350°.

Fill shucked oysters with mixture and bake until lightly
toasted, about ten minutes.

Lamb Chop Medallions on Creamy Spinach Gnocchi with Shaved Parmesan, Port Wine Reduction

Serves 2

Lamb Medallions

Preheat oven to 350°

1 lamb rib roast, bones and sinew removed from loin
2 Tbsp. chopped fresh herb mix of thyme, rosemary,
and mint
1 egg white, beat until foamy

Season lamb loin with salt and black pepper and sear in a hot skillet with olive oil until skin is blistered and browned. Set the loin aside to cool and brush it lightly with the egg whites and then coat with fresh chopped herbs. Cook in oven until meat feels firm. Remove from oven and allow to rest for 5 minutes before slicing into 6 uniform medallions. Salt and pepper.

Creamy Spinach Gnocchi
Preheat oven to 350°.
1 pound russet potatoes
1 to 1¼ cups flour
2 egg yolks
2 Tbsp. spinach purée, cook 1 bunch of spinach until wilted
  and blend in a blender until smooth
1 tsp. salt
¼ cup heavy whipping cream
2 Tbsp. fresh butter
1 cup shaved parmesan (shave with a vegetable peeler)
Salt and pepper

Bake potatoes until soft and pass them through a ricer or a sieve. While they are still hot, sprinkle flour, egg yolks, spinach purée, and salt over them. Working quickly, cut the mixture together with a rubber spatula until the mixture comes together and forms a ball. Roll the ball in a bit of flour and divide into 2 portions. Roll each portion on a lightly floured surface to form a "snake" about ½ inch thick. Cut the snake into pieces about 1 inch long and flatten halfway with the tines of a fork. Blanch the pieces in a simmering pot of salted water until they float to the top. Remove the gnocchi and place them in a skillet with the butter, cream, half of the parmesan, and the salt and pepper. Toss to coat.

Port Wine Reduction
2 cups Port wine
1 shallot, minced

Heat the shallot with the Port until reduced by two-thirds.

Blanched Asparagus Tips

Blanch asparagus in salted water until tender.

To Plate: Place one portion of the gnocchi on the bottom half of the plate. Place 3 lamb medallions on the upper half of the plate and drizzle with Port wine reduction and sprinkle remaining shaved parmesan over the gnocchi. Garnish with asparagus tips.

White Chocolate and Pistachio Crême Brûlée with Cherry Compote
6 servings

Brûlée recipe
5 egg yolks
½ cup sugar + 3 Tbsp. reserved
1 vanilla bean, scraped
2 cups heavy whipping cream
4 oz. white chocolate, melted
½ tsp. pistachio extract
6 tsp. sugar for torching

51

In a stainless steel bowl, whisk ¼ cup sugar into egg yolks until sugar is dissolved. Heat cream, scraped vanilla bean and ¼ cup sugar to a simmer. Whisk the hot cream mixture into the egg mixture and then mix in the melted chocolate and pistachio extract, remove vanilla bean.

Place six 8-oz. ceramic ramekins in a deep pan and divide the mixture among them, leaving room at the top. Fill the pan halfway up the sides of the ramekins with hot water and place in hot oven. Bake until the custards are set, about 30 minutes. Cool the custards in the refrigerator for at least 4 hours. Sprinkle 1 tsp. sugar over the top of each of the 6 custards and torch until the sugar hardens (you can use your broiler).

Cherry Compote
4 cups cherries, fresh and pitted
1½ cups sugar
1 orange, zested and juiced

Heat all ingredients in a stainless steel pot and cook over medium heat until the mixture turns to a syrup and coats the back of a spoon. Cool and spoon over the top of the crème brûlées. Garnish with whipped cream, crushed pistachios, and mint tips. Serve immediately.

Matt Martinez

Matt's Rancho Martinez, Dallas

Mex Tex: Traditional Tex-Mex Taste

Tex-Mex. It's the food we all know—lunch special #1, cheese enchiladas, beans and rice; lunch special #5, spinach quesadilla with cheese; lunch special #10, chicken flauta, chicken enchilada with sour cream sauce, beans, and rice. And, ah, add iced tea—or maybe a good cold beer—to that order.

Matt Martinez takes Tex-Mex a step away from what we're all used to—and a step back in history. Saying there's a world of confusion and misunderstanding about what Tex-Mex is or isn't, this fourth-generation Tex-Mex chef says that it is the peasant food of the Southwest, celebrating history, spirit, texture, and just plain good eating.

Tex-Mex can trace its origins back to the 1500s, when the Indians and Spanish collided—and mixed their cooking traditions. Then the ingredients may have been jackrabbit or armadillo, wild onion, pepper, cactus leaves—whatever was handy. The challenge of cooking with local ingredients brought out the best in the cooks and created a cuisine that reflects those pioneers. They made something out of nothing, in the American western tradition of "making do."

The chili queens of San Antonio first made this style of cooking popular. After the Civil War, they were the women who made chili in their homes and took it in colorful wagons to San Antonio's Haymarket, Alamo, and Military plazas. They kept it warm over mesquite fires. In the late 1800s, Military Plaza, now the city of San Antonio's city hall, was known as La Plaza del Chili Con Carne.

Matt Martinez' Mex Tex has no abundance of exotic spices, meats, or vegetables. There are not the infusions, reductions, and presentations of other cuisines. "The infusion came 500 years ago, with the Spanish and Indian migrants," he says, claiming there have been few changes in the last hundred years. Today the ingredients are more convenient; the spices, meats, and vegetables more readily available. Haven't you noticed tomatillos in your grocery store in the last ten years?

Sauces, according to Martinez, are the lifeblood of Tex-Mex cuisine—red chile, ranchero, green sauce, hot sauce. Cream and queso sauces are "Johnny-come-lately."

Matt Martinez' father opened Matt's El Rancho in Austin in 1952, and young Matt worked in the kitchen. At first he was in charge of salads and appetizers. He recalls one night when politician Bob Armstrong walked into the kitchen and said, "Little Matt, give me something different for an appetizer … something not on the menu."

"Little Matt" told him to go sit down, the appetizer was on its way. But in truth he had no idea what he was going to do. He began grabbing ingredients—taco meat, guacamole, sour cream. Then he poured chile con queso over the top and put the whole thing in the oven. By the next day customers were ordering "that Bob Armstrong dip that's not on the menu." Little Matt was off fishing, and the rest of the staff had no idea what was in this secret concoction. Now it's a staple on his menu. ★

Bob Armstrong's Dip
    Traditional guacamole
    Taco meat
    Chile con queso

Warm a 9 x 13 inch pan. Spread guacamole into the pan, then add a layer of hot taco meat. Top with hot chile con queso. Serve with chips, chalupa shells, or tortillas. Garnish with pico, sour cream, or your favorite hot sauce.

Tex-Mex Spice
Use this with chili, taco meat, rice, sauces, and so on. Brown slightly during cooking process. Matt uses it for most of his dishes.
    3 Tbsp. plus 2 tsp. ground cumin
    3 Tbsp. granulated garlic
    2 Tbsp.salt
    1 Tbsp. coarsely ground black pepper

Early Texas Turkey Chili Indian-Style
    Serves 4

    1 lb. ground turkey; wild turkey has more flavor;
    ground pork also works well.
    1½ Tbsp. cooking oil
    1½ Tbsp. cornstarch
    1 Tbsp. chili powder
    1 large garlic clove, sliced
    2 tsp. dried leaf oregano
    1 can (14-½ oz.) whole or stewed tomatoes
    1 cup fresh or frozen corn
    1 cup finely chopped zucchini
    ¼ cup coarsely chopped sweet white onion
    ¼ cup coarsely chopped canned green chiles or bell pepper
    2 whole chipotle peppers in adobo sauce or 1 Tbsp. thinly
    sliced hot peppers.
    1 cup chicken broth

Using a cast-iron or nonstick skillet or pot, sauté the turkey in oil for 2-3 minutes. Add cornstarch, chili powder, garlic, and oregano; sauté for 2-3 minutes. Add vegetables, peppers and broth. Simmer approximately 5-10 minutes. Adjust seasoning to taste and serve immediately.

Wino Quail
Serves 4-6

4 Tbsp. butter
6 whole quail or 8 quail breasts
3 Tbsp. flour
¾ tsp. salt
½ tsp. white pepper
2 cups coarsely chopped onions
2 cups coarsely chopped mushrooms
3 cloves garlic, thinly sliced
⅛ tsp. thyme leaves
1 cup chicken broth
1 cup white wine
1 cup half-and-half or heavy cream
Chopped chives or parsley to garnish

In Dutch oven or other large pot, melt butter over moderate heat. Dust quail with flour, salt, and pepper, then place in pot. Add onions, mushrooms, garlic, and thyme. Toss and scrape the birds along with other ingredients in the pot for 3 to 4 minutes, cooking until onions are translucent.

Add the broth and wine. Cook gently with lid on for 1 to 1-½ hours, watching the broth so it does not get dry. Add water as needed, and occasionally scrape the bottom of the pot. If the sauce is too thick, you may also add water until you reach the desired consistency.

When the birds are tender, add cream and simmer gently for 3 to 4 minutes. Season with salt and pepper to taste. Garnish with chives or parsley. Serve over rice.

★

Stephan Pyles
Stephan Pyles Restaurant, Dallas

SAY THE NAME STEPHAN PYLES IN DALLAS, and most people recall their favorite dish from Routh Street Café or Baby Routh, the spectacular Star Canyon of the '90s with its in-your-face cowboy atmosphere, or AquaKnox, which he described as a "global" seafood restaurant. Stephan Pyles has opened over a dozen restaurants in the last twenty-two years, most but not all in the Dallas area, and then, in time, moved on from each.

In the first part of the twenty-first century, he spent his time traveling and researching, consulting, writing, teaching, and producing television cooking shows. But, he says, something was missing. The "something" was a restaurant, and in the fall of 2005, he opened the restaurant bearing his name, Stephan Pyles. Now, he jokes that having his name on a restaurant is a bit scary but investors thought it "branded" the establishment.

Pyles, a native of West Texas, is often hailed as a pioneer of New American Cuisine and the father of Southwestern Cuisine. Certainly, he has changed the cooking scene in Texas, upgrading the West Texas and Mexican tastes of his childhood to sophisticated gourmet cuisine. He grew up working at his family's truck-stop café in Big Spring and is a self-taught chef. "Nothing is new," he says, "just new ways of putting things together."

The new restaurant features what the chef describes as New Millennium Southwestern Cuisine. The menu has more global inspiration, bringing in the Middle Eastern and Mediterranean tastes that are inherent in the cuisine of Spain, which has a major influence on Pyles' current cooking, and it shows an innovative ability to combine unusual flavors. Going for lunch? Try the Southwestern Caesar Salad, a dish from Star Canyon that features ancho chiles in the dressing and croutons of fried squares of jalapeño polenta. Want a sandwich? How about Hickory Smoked Barbecued Pork on a Black Pepper Biscuit with Horseradish Crema, or a Lobster Salad Club with Smoked "Duck Bacon" and Meyer Lemon Mayonnaise. Dinner? Start with a variety of Peruvian ceviches, then move on perhaps to Seared Foie Gras "Tacu Tacu" with Lentils and Bananas—the foie gras is put on a caramelized banana slice and the whole set on a "cake" of lentils and rice; then the pan is deglazed with a sweet Spanish sherry, and brown poultry stock finishes the sauce. Or maybe you'd like a Tamale Tart with

Roast Garlic Custard and Jumbo Lump Crabmeat and Smoky Tomato Sauce.

Stephan Pyles (the restaurant, not the man) shows a much more subtle Southwestern influence in its décor than did Star Canyon. Its red terra cotta wall tiles were part of the original building. Decorators, with Pyles' input, added thin slices of Texas limestone, a wood ceiling, and metal grilles and screens to subdivide the space. The lighting slowly changes colors, exposing the brick walls. A partially open kitchen is in the center, and guests can watch food preparation on a large screen plasma TV (makes the restaurant a cooking bar instead of a sports bar in a way).

Pyles' creations have brought him numerous awards—the first Texan inducted into The James Beard Foundation's *Who's Who of Food and Beverage in America; Esquire* magazine's Chef of the Year in 2006; one of the "twenty most impressive, intriguing, and influential Texans for 1998" according to *Texas Monthly;* in 2007, the same magazine named Stephan Pyles the best new restaurant of the year. The list is endless. Pyles' cookbooks are *The New Texas Cuisine, Tamales, Southwestern Vegetarian and New Tastes from Texas,* which was the companion piece to a twenty-six-part, Emmy Award-winning PBS cooking series.

Stephan Pyles believes in giving back, and he is known for his philanthropic work. He is a founding board member of Share Our Strength, an international hunger relief organization, which presented him with its distinguished Humanitarian of the Year award in 1998. He's a life board member of the North Texas Food Bank and founded Dallas' Taste of the Nation, a fundraiser for local ministries and food pantries. A co-founder of The Hunger Link, which links restaurants and hotels with shelters and other food programs, he offers a $15,000 annual scholarship through the Texas Hill Country Wine and Food Foundation to a rising culinary star in Texas. ★

Tamale Tart with Roast Garlic Custard and Gulf Crabmeat
Serves 8 -10

For the Roast Garlic Custard:
3 cups heavy cream
3 Tbsp. puréed roasted garlic
4 egg yolks
2 tsp. salt
¼ tsp. freshly ground white pepper

For the Tart shell:
1 large red bell pepper, seeded and coarsely chopped
2 cups masa harina
¼ cup yellow cornmeal
¼ tsp. cayenne powder
2 tsp. ground cumin
2 tsp. salt
6 Tbsp. vegetable shortening, at room temperature
6 Tbsp. ancho chile purée
2 cups water

For the Crabmeat topping:
2 Tbsp. olive oil
½ small onion, finely chopped
10 oz. fresh lump crabmeat

>>>>>>>>>>

¼ cup red tomato, blanched, peeled, seeded, and diced
¼ cup yellow tomato, blanched, peeled, seeded, and diced
2 Tbsp. chopped cilantro
1 serrano chile, seeded and minced
2 tsp. fresh lime juice
Salt to taste

To prepare the Garlic Custard:

Place the cream in a medium saucepan over medium heat and reduce to 1 cup plus 2 Tbsp. Whisk in the roasted garlic. In a mixing bowl, whisk the egg yolks lightly while drizzling in the cream mixture, and season with salt and pepper. Cover and set aside to cool.

To prepare the Tart:

Steam the red bell pepper over boiling water until soft, about 10 minutes. Drain and transfer to a blender or food processor; blend until smooth. You should have about ¾ cup purée; if necessary, add a little water to make up the quantity.

In a medium bowl, combine the masa harina, cornmeal, cayenne, cumin, and salt. In a large bowl, using an electric mixer at medium speed, whip the shortening until light and fluffy.

Gradually beat in the dry ingredients until smooth. Beat in the ancho chile purée and the red bell pepper purée. Form the dough into a disk, and pat into a 9-inch tart pan with a removable bottom, pressing the dough evenly over the bottom and up the sides. Fill the tart pan with the reserved garlic custard and cover with plastic wrap.

Place a round metal cooling rack inside a wok and pour in the 2 cups water. The rack should fit at least 3 inches above the water. Bring the water to a boil over high heat, then turn off the heat. Place the wrapped tart on the rack and reheat the water until it boils again. Lower the heat to simmer, cover the wok, and steam until the custard is set but still trembles slightly, 25 to 30 minutes. Using 2 potholders, carefully lift the tart off the rack; remove the plastic wrap and the sides of the tart ring. Transfer to a serving platter.

In a large non-reactive skillet, heat the olive oil over high heat, until lightly smoking. Add the onion and cook, stirring for 1 minute. Stir in the crabmeat, tomatoes, cilantro, serrano, and lime juice, and cook until warmed through, about 2 minutes. Season with salt. Using a slotted spoon, cover the top of the tart with the crab mixture. Cut the tart into wedges and serve warm.

Rock Shrimp Taquitos with Mango Barbecue and Avocado Salsa
Yields 16

For the Taquitos:
1 Tbsp. olive oil
1 pound rock shrimp, peeled and deveined
½ medium onion, diced
½ cup red bell pepper, seeded and diced
½ cup yellow bell pepper, seeded and diced
½ cup poblano, seeded and diced
½ cup shredded Chihuahua cheese
3 Tbsp. chopped fresh cilantro
2 Tbsp. ancho purée
Salt to taste
16 flour tortillas, cut into 4" circles and warmed

Heat the oil in a large sauté pan until lightly smoking. Add the shrimp, onion, bell peppers, and poblano; sauté for 2 minutes. Remove from the heat and stir in cheese, cilantro, and ancho purée. Season with salt.

Place a heaping Tbsp. of the shrimp mixture on half of each tortilla, then fold over like a quesadilla. Serve with Mango Barbecue Sauce and garnish with Avocado Salsa.

Mango Barbecue Sauce
1 Tbsp. olive oil
1 medium onion, diced
2 cloves garlic, chopped
1 habañero, stemmed, seeded, and chopped
2 Tbsp. cider vinegar
1 Tbsp. light brown sugar
1 Tbsp. pasilla purée
1 mango, peeled, pitted, and puréed
1 cup chicken stock
juice of 2 limes
juice of 1 orange
1 Tbsp. dry mustard
1 Tbsp. Dijon mustard
Salt to taste

Heat the oil in a small saucepan over medium heat until lightly smoking. Add the onion and sauté for 1 minute. Add the garlic and habañero and continue to cook about 2–3 minutes or until the onion is translucent, stirring occasionally.

Add the vinegar, sugar, and pasilla purée; cook until thick, about three minutes. Add the mango purée and chicken stock. Reduce the heat to low and simmer for 10 minutes. Whisk in the lime juice, orange juice and dry mustard and Dijon; simmer for 3–5 more minutes. Strain through a fine sieve, salt to taste, and serve with the taquitos.

Avocado-Tomatillo Salsa (makes about 1½ cups)
2 large avocados, peeled, pitted, and diced
1 tsp. red bell pepper, diced
1 tsp. green bell pepper, diced
1 Tbsp. scallions, diced
4 medium tomatillos, husked and diced
1 clove garlic, minced
2 Tbsp. chopped fresh cilantro
2 serrano chiles, seeded and diced
2 tsp. fresh lime juice
3 Tbsp. olive oil
Salt to taste

Combine the avocados, bell peppers, scallion, and half of the tomatillos in a large mixing bowl; set aside. Place the garlic, cilantro, serranos, lime juice, and remaining tomatillos in a blender and purée until smooth. Slowly drizzle in the olive oil. Add the purée to the avocado mixture; combine thoroughly, and season with salt. Let stand for at least 30 minutes before serving. Serve chilled.

Salmon Ceviche with Capers, Green Olives and Jalapeños

Serves 4

For the Roasted Tomato Salsa:

4 ripe tomatoes
1 yellow onion, peeled and cut into quarters
4 mashed garlic cloves
1 red bell pepper
1 jalapeño
Salt to taste

For the Ceviche:

12 oz. salmon filet, skin removed and meat cut into 1 inch by
    ½ inch strips
4 tsp. key lime juice
Salt to taste (about 2 tsp.)
2 Tbsp. drained capers
2 Tbsp. chopped pitted green olives
1 Tbsp. chopped cilantro
1 jalapeño, seeded and minced
½ cup roasted tomato salsa
Preheat oven to 450°.

For the tomato salsa:

Toss all items except fish and lime juice with small amount of olive oil and season with salt and place on a baking sheet. Place in the oven and roast until peppers and onions are a deep brown color, approximately 15 minutes. Remove from oven and cool. Peel and seed the chiles and peppers. Place meat of peppers and all remaining items, including the juice on the baking sheet, into a blender and purée until smooth. Taste, adjust seasoning with salt, taste again. Chill the salsa before mixing the ceviche.

To make the ceviche:

Place the salmon in a glass or stainless steel bowl and add the lime juice and salt. Let the ceviche marinate for 5 minutes, then add the remaining ingredients and mix well.

Serve well chilled. ★

Miguel Ravago

Fonda San Miguel, Austin

Fonda San Miguel: Thirty Years of Food and Art

You'd expect Miguel Ravago to be a native of Mexico, but he's not. He was born and raised in Phoenix, but he often visited northern Mexico where his family had many relatives. In Phoenix, his grandmother cooked for the entire extended family. There were

FONDA SAN MIGUEL
Thirty Years of Food and Art

TOM GILLILAND AND MIGUEL RAVAGO
Text by Virginia B. Wood

often, he recalls, twenty people at the table. Cooking was his grandmother's avocation, and since she was part Spanish, her cooking showed a heavy Spanish influence. She, too, went often to Mexico and brought back ideas and ingredients.

Always curious, Miguel began to help his grandmother in the kitchen as a young child. He was, he thinks, six or seven when he learned to fill tamales. By then, he was helping quite a bit. Gradually he took over the cooking for the entire family, and then he knew he wanted to be a chef.

When he left home, his first job was in Houston, working for Neiman Marcus. Because he was bilingual, he helped entertain guests from Mexico, taking them to Mexican restaurants. But he never found food like his grandmother had taught him to cook. Although he never attended culinary school, he took some cooking lessons and spent two weeks in New York, working with Diana Kennedy.

Arguably the grande dame of Mexican cuisine, Kennedy was born in the United Kingdom but moved to Mexico in 1957 with her husband. Widowed, she stayed on and has spent more than forty-five years traveling through Mexico and researching its food. The author of several cookbooks, she was awarded the Order of the Aztec Eagle (the equivalent of knighthood for non-Mexicans) for her work in preserving Mexican cuisine. When Miguel worked with her, he went off with a grocery list every morning. When he returned, they cooked—and then gave the food to neighbors. Miguel recalls that mostly he learned, but he was able to tell her a few things his grandmother did. His mentoring relationship with her, which began in Houston, has lasted almost forty years.

He also attended workshops with other chefs, learned to use non-traditional ingredients, and to be flexible, substituting when needed.

In 1972, he and business partner Tom Gilliland opened

San Angel in Houston, a small restaurant—50 seats—serving authentic cuisines from the interior of Mexico. Miguel figured that the general public knew Tex-Mex food, but they didn't know chipotle chiles and black beans. Houston society found them, and the restaurant was a success. By the mid-1970s, they needed a bigger place.

Miguel and Gilliland opted for Austin and found a large stucco building that had housed a restaurant called Mi Casa Es Su Casa, located in a residential neighborhood. In 1975, they opened Fonda San Miguel in a city full of outstanding restaurants, with more than its share of Tex-Mex and barbecue places. They flew in the face of existing Mexican restaurants— there was, Miguel reminds, no Enchilada Plate Number One. Some clients walked out because they expected Tex-Mex. But thanks to numerous politicians, prime among them Lyndon Baines Johnson, the restaurant flourished.

Fonda San Miguel's mission was to educate the public, to introduce them to ingredients they'd not tasted before. At first it was difficult, and produce particularly had to be imported from Mexico. But gradually local sources began to supply chipotle and poblano chiles, tomatillos, black beans, epazote, and other delicacies.

Two things beside the menu distinguish Fonda San Miguel: one is the art that decorates the restaurant. The atmosphere of Mexico is enhanced by statuary, ceramics, pottery, folk art, fabrics, and museum quality paintings. Tom Gilliland travels to Mexico to buy works from the best known and most intriguing artists. He operates on instinct and is not so much thinking of building a collection as he is of decorating the restaurant, changing its appearance from time to time. The partners estimate that they have more art stored than hangs on the wall. But they rotate the works, so that the restaurant always looks new and different. Menus, too, reflect Mexican art—they were designed by Mexican designers, using original Mexican art.

Perhaps the most distinguishing feature of the restaurant's week is the Sunday brunch at the hacienda. Tables are set in a large rectangle in the center of the restaurant and decorated with Mexican fabrics, pottery, and fresh fruit and flowers. Miguel stands in the center of that rectangle, greeting customers, answering their questions, telling them about the food. Diners find imaginative hot and cold dishes—huevos rancheros like none you've ever tasted before, huevos en rabo de mestizo (eggs poached in a Mexican sauce), chilaquiles de Guajolote (tortilla casserole with turkey), chipotle potato gratin, escabeche de verdures (pickled vegetables). Salads may have fresh flowers tossed among their ingredients.

The flowers come from the extensive gardens surrounding Fonda San Miguel. For cooking, Miguel simply wanders in the garden to see what's fresh and looks good that day—herbs to cook with, perhaps pansies for the salads, banana leaves in which to wrap fish so that the oils spread into the cooking meat (the grounds have seventy-five banana trees). For the beans, perhaps epazote, a strong wild herb with a taste like coriander (it's said to reduce gas)—or maybe it's rosemary, thyme, marjoram, anise, or hoja santa, a fragrant plant called "sacred leaf," and often used for tamales or to wrap fish and meats. He stresses that no pesticides are ever used in the gardens.

Miguel has twice been invited to present an event at the James Beard House in New York and has recreated the Sunday buffet.

The path has not always been smooth. In 1985, Miguel and Tom opened a second restaurant in Houston. It coincided with the great bust of Texas finances and was, they say, a bad financial experience that put the Austin restaurant in danger.

In 1995, they dissolved their partnership, and Miguel took

over as chef at Bertram's by Miguel in downtown Austin. He found, to his chagrin, that the backers wanted his name but not his authentic food. He left for Santa Fe and then New York City. Other chefs took over at Fonda San Miguel, introducing nueva cocina—Mexican cooking using French fusion techniques. By 2000, Miguel was back in Austin—he didn't like high-rise living in New York. He was chef for a catering company that folded with the dot.com crash. He went to see Tom Gilliland and was hired as co-manager. Soon the chef left, and Miguel was back where he belongs—in the kitchen of Fonda San Miguel.

★

Sopa de Tortilla
      Serves 6

Miguel modeled his tortilla soup on that famous at the restaurant Fonda El Pato in Mexico City.

      6 Tbsp. vegetable oil
      12 small corn tortillas, cut into ¼ inch strips
      2 medium tomatoes, broiled
      ¼ cup chopped white onion
      1 garlic clove
      6 cups chicken broth, preferably homemade
      Sea salt and ground pepper to taste
      2 sprigs fresh epazote, chopped, or 2 Tbsp. dried
      6 Tbsp. shredded Monterey Jack cheese
      2 dried pasilla chiles, fried crisp (10-15 seconds), seeded and crumbled

Heat oil in heavy Dutch oven. Fry tortilla strips until golden brown (2-3 minutes); remove with slotted spoon, drain and set aside. Pour off all but 1 Tbsp. oil in the pan and set aside. In a blender, combine tomatoes, onion, and garlic. Purée. Heat remaining Tbsp. of oil over medium heat and fry the puréed sauce until it has thickened and is reduced by about one-quarter. Add chicken broth and bring to a boil. Check seasonings, adding salt and pepper. Reduce to simmer and add half the tortilla strips and the epazote. Cook 5 minutes.

      Serve by dividing remaining tortilla strips among 6 bowls and putting 1 Tbsp. of shredded cheese into each one. Ladle hot soup into the bowls and garnish with crumbled chiles.

Camarones al Mojo de Ajo (Shrimp in Garlic Sauce)
      Serves 6

      ¾ cup butter
      3 garlic cloves, thinly sliced
      ⅓ cup olive oil
      36 raw shrimp (21-25 count), peeled and deveined
      Chopped fresh parsley for garnish

Fried Garlic
1 cup vegetable oil
¾ cup minced garlic

Prepare fried garlic first. In heavy skillet, heat oil over high heat until shimmering but not smoking. Add garlic, reduce heat to medium-low, and cook 10 to 15 minutes or until golden brown, stirring often. (Be careful not to burn.) Remove garlic from oil with slotted spoon, strain through a fine strainer, and drain on paper towels.

In small saucepan, melt butter over medium heat; add the sliced garlic, reduce heat to low, and keep warm on top of the stove. Do not brown the garlic. In nonreactive skillet or sauté pan, heat the olive oil over medium-high heat and sauté the shrimp until they curl and turn pink, 4-5 minutes. Divide shrimp among 6 dinner plates and spoon the warm garlic butter sauce over each serving. Sprinkle with fried garlic and chopped parsley. Serve with Arroz Blanco.

Arroz Blanco (White rice)
Serves 8

2 Tbsp. safflower oil
2 cups long-grain white rice
4 cups chicken broth
1 tsp. sea salt or to taste
1 cup frozen green peas, thawed

Heat oil in heavy 3-qt. saucepan or Dutch oven over medium-high heat. Add rice, stirring often with a wooden spoon. Cook 8-10 minutes or until rice is golden. Add chicken broth, reduce heat to medium, cover and cook 20 minutes or until all liquid has been absorbed. Fluff with a fork and add salt, if necessary. Sprinkle with green peas and serve hot.

Terry Thompson-Anderson

http://www.thetexasfoodandwinegourmet.com

Texas on the Plate

TERRY THOMPSON-ANDERSON DOESN'T HAVE A RESTAURANT, glitzy or rustic or otherwise. But she's owned her own restaurant, served as a chef for a private executive resort, and owned a cooking school. Today, she is the author of three cookbooks and a consultant, cooking teacher, cooking demonstrator, lecturer at food events, and the spirit behind a line of specialty sauces and products. She relies on French techniques but describes herself as a rustic gourmet. Her cooking is heavily influenced by traditional southern cooking, French infusion techniques, the bold seasoning of Cajun foods, and, in the last decade or so, the wild game and other local products available in Texas.

Thompson-Anderson was raised in Houston by a mother who did not cook. As a young adult with a BA in English, she found herself a bride who didn't know how to cook for her husband. But his mother was a wonderful southern cook who took her new daughter-in-law under her wing. The young woman discovered food in the kitchen and even got to the point where she could make her own mayonnaise. Fascinated by food, she ignored her weight gain and kept cooking. When she and her husband moved to Austin, she took cooking classes designed for women for whom cooking was a hobby. Then the couple was transferred to Louisiana, and she began teaching classes at a small shop in Covington.

English degree aside, she decided to study cooking seriously, mostly because her husband suggested she either had to stop cooking on such a grand scale or get paid for it. She had met and studied with Nathalie Dupree, a southern cook, television cooking personality, and author of *Southern Memories*. Dupree sponsored Terry as a member of the International Association of Culinary Professionals. Next came study at L'Academie de Cuisine in Bethesda, Maryland, where she studied the classic French curriculum. "If you're going to get into food," she says, "you have to learn French techniques because they are the basis of all cuisine." She went on to study privately with several chefs and at the Beringer School of Professional Chefs at Beringer Winery in Napa Valley. She even spent an intensive week, along with five other professionals, studying with James Beard at the Stanford Court Hotel kitchens in San Francisco.

In 1979 in Lafayette, Louisiana, Terry founded Cooking, Inc. Her school was featured in *Bon Appetit,* which led to requests for classes from students all over this country and some from Europe. She began to do staff training and menu development for restaurants across the country and met new cooking colleagues. Among those she notes are Cajun chefs

Paul Prudhomme and Emeril Lagasse.

Terry opened her own restaurant, Café Raintree, in Bay St. Louis, Mississippi, in 1986. The menu included contemporary Cajun, Creole, and southern dishes. In 1991, because of personal circumstances, she closed the restaurant and moved back to Houston to become executive chef for the Halliburton Corporation. She was the chef at the corporation's Manor Lake Lodge in West Columbia, Brazoria County. As such she chose the menu, ordered the food, hired and trained the staff, and oversaw all aspects of food service at the private hunting and fishing lodge/conference center. It was there she began to concentrate on game.

The Halliburton people wanted food typical of Texas because they entertained people from all over the world. Thompson-Anderson had little experience with game, but she learned, she says, by doing. She made rattlesnake chili, cooked quail with country ham in a peppered coffee gravy and served it on Cajun-style dirty rice (white rice cooked with chicken livers and gizzards). She learned to cook venison, wild boar, rabbit, and antelope. Sometimes she used smoked hog jowls as a seasoning meat, a technique learned from the cooking of poor southerners. Once she experimented and made chicken-fried rib-eye steak. It still needs cream gravy, according to Thompson-Anderson, but it is a departure from the usual chicken-fried steak.

"Fat," she says, "makes food taste good, and as a chef, the challenge is to make food that tastes good."

Her three cookbooks are *Cajun-Creole Cooking, Eating Southern Style,* and *Texas on the Plate.* She is at work on *Texas Hill Country: A Food and Wine Lover's Paradise,* due out in the fall of 2008.

You can see Thompson-Anderson's line of food products (produced by Fischer & Wieser Specialty Foods), read about her thoughts on Texas food, and find some of her recipes online at http://www.thetexasfoodandwinegourmet.com.

Following are some of Terry Thompson-Anderson's favorite recipes. ★

Avocado Cream Soup with Lime and Chili Tortilla Strips
Serves 8 –10

This great chilled soup tastes like the very essence of summer in Texas. It's sultry and spicy, smooth with crispy highlights, and it will make you feel good—just like summer in Texas. It was first developed as a recipe for a winery luncheon at Spicewood Vineyard as part of the 2003 Texas Hill Country Food and Wine Festival.

> 4 ripe Haas avocados, peeled, seeded and cut in 1-inch cubes
> ½ cup firmly packed cilantro leaves and tender top stems
> 3 serrano chilies, seeds and veins removed, roughly chopped
> 1 quart good quality chicken stock
> 1 cup whipping cream
> ¼ cup freshly squeezed lime juice
> Salt to taste
> Sour cream

Lime and Chili Tortilla Strips:
Chopped cilantro leaves
Tiny Dice Pico De Gallo, see recipe on next page
Lime and Chili Tortilla Strips
10 white corn tortillas, cut in half, then cut into strips about ¼ inch wide.
Canola oil for deep-frying, heated to 350°
2 Tbsp. good quality chili powder
Lime-flavored "beer" salt, or substitute plain sea salt

To make the Lime and Chili Tortilla strips:
Fry the tortilla strips in preheated oil until crisp and very lightly browned, about 2-3 minutes. Drain on wire racks and set aside. Remove the seeds from the serrano chilies and toast the chilies in a dry cast iron skillet over medium-high heat until they are very crisp. Do not burn the chilis. Grind the chilies to a powder in a spice mill or coffee grinder. Toss the chili powder with some of the lime salt in a small bowl, blending well. Season the fried tortilla strips liberally with the chili powder mixture. The tortilla strips should be dark in color from the powder. Store in container with tight-fitting lid until ready to use.

Tiny Dice Pico de Gallo
5 Roma tomatoes, cut into tiny dice, about ¼-inch square
2 serrano chilies, seeds and veins removed, minced
¼ cup finely diced onion
2 Tbsp. chopped cilantro
2 tsp. lime juice
Salt to taste

Combine all ingredients except salt in a small bowl and toss to blend well. Season to taste with the salt and refrigerate until ready to use.

To prepare soup:
Combine the avocado, cilantro, serrano chilies and 1½ cups of the chicken stock in blender. Process until mixture is very smooth. Transfer to a medium-sized bowl and whisk in the remaining chicken stock, whipping cream, and lime juice. Add salt to taste and whisk to blend well. Taste for seasoning, adding additional salt if the soup tastes "flat" and boring. Cover and refrigerate until well chilled before serving.

To serve, ladle a portion of the soup into each soup bowl, then top with a dollop of sour cream. Nest a bunch of the Lime and Chili Tortilla Strips on the sour cream, then scatter some of the chopped cilantro and Tiny Dice Pico De Gallo over the tortilla strips.

Note: There is an art to seasoning foods which will be served cold, such as this soup. Cold dulls the senses of hot, sweet, salty, and spicy on our tongues. Therefore, you should slightly over-season foods that will be served cold, or they will taste very bland once they have been refrigerated. After the food has been chilled it is very hard to adjust the seasonings. A good example of how this little phenomenon works is to think about the times you may have tasted melted ice cream. Remember how extremely sweet it tasted? Yet when it was frozen, it was just perfect. Ice cream is over-sweetened before freezing, so that it will be just right once it is frozen. So don't be stingy with the salt in this soup, or it just won't reach its full flavor potential.

When choosing avocados be sure to purchase the small Haas avocados with dark, bumpy skins. This avocado has flourished in the lush countryside of Michoacan, west of Mexico City, for thousands of years. The avocados should never be hard but should yield slightly to the touch. Reject those that are very soft and squishy. To open an avocado, cut lengthwise around the pit, and gently twist the two halves to separate. Strike the pit with the blade of a sharp knife, then twist to remove the seed. With a spoon, scoop out the avocado flesh.

Quail in Country Ham with Peppered Coffee Gravy on Dirty Rice
Serves 6

12 semi-boneless quail (backbone and breastbone removed)
Melted unsalted butter
Salt and freshly ground black pepper
12 thin-cut Smithfield country-cured ham slices

Preheat oven to 350°. Brush each quail liberally with some of the melted butter. Season with salt and freshly ground black pepper. Wrap each quail in a slice of the ham, leaving the wings exposed on top of the ham slice. Place the quail in a single layer in a heavy baking pan with the loose ends of the ham slices tucked underneath. Roast in preheated oven for 45 minutes or until quail are just cooked through.

Dirty Rice
1 pound chicken or turkey gizzards
½ pound chicken, duck or turkey livers
1 cup bacon or sausage drippings (or substitute solid
  vegetable shortening)
2 medium onions, chopped
1 green bell pepper, chopped
2 celery stalks, chopped, including leafy tops
2 garlic cloves, minced
3 cups chicken stock
½ tsp. cayenne pepper or to taste
Salt and freshly ground pepper to taste
¼ cup minced flat-leaf parsley
5 green onions chopped, including green tops
4 cups cooked white rice

Prepare the dirty rice while the quail are roasting. Using a small, sharp knife, remove the tough outer skin from the gizzards by scraping the meat from the skin, leaving the blade of the knife against the skin on the cutting board. Place the gizzards and livers in the work bowl of food processor fitted with steel blade and process to purée the meats. Scrape the purée out of the bowl with rubber spatula and set aside.

Heat the drippings in a heavy 12-inch frying pan over medium-high heat. When the fat is hot, add the puréed meats and cook, stirring often, until well browned. Be sure the meat does not cook into clumps. Add the onion, bell pepper, garlic, and celery, blending well. Cook until vegetables are wilted, about 8 minutes. Add the stock and seasonings, scraping the bottom of the pan to release any browned bits of meat glaze. Cook over medium heat until liquid is reduced and thickened, about 45 minutes. Stir in parsley, green onions, and rice, mixing well. Cook, stirring often, for about 10 minutes, or until rice is slightly sticky.

Peppered Coffee Gravy
½ cup bacon drippings (or solid vegetable shortening)
2 Smithfield country-cured ham slices, ¼ inch thick
1 tsp. freshly ground black pepper
4 Tbsp. all purpose flour
1 cup strong black coffee
1½ cup beef stock

While quail and rice are cooking, prepare the gravy. Heat bacon drippings in a heavy 10-inch cast-iron skillet over medium heat. Add the ham slices and cook until they are very crisp. Remove and set aside. Add the pepper and flour to the bacon drippings, stir to blend well. Cook for about 5 minutes, stirring constantly, to give the gravy greater depth of flavor. Add the coffee and stir rapidly to blend well. Bring to a boil and cook for 3 to 4 minutes. Stir in the beef stock. Chop the reserved ham slices into crumb-size pieces and add to the gravy. Cook, stirring, until thickened.

To serve, place a bed of dirty rice in the center of each serving plate. Next put two quail in the center and spoon a portion of gravy over the quail. Serve hot.

Shiner Bock Rice Pilaf
Serves 4–6

Next time you're looking for a great side dish to go with grilled red meat or pork, give this bold-flavored pilaf a try. PLEASE don't use a wimpy beer to make the recipe. Shiner Bock has a special flavor nuance that creates the perfect taste in this recipe. Besides, it's supporting Texas when you use Shiner Beer! We also love to use Texmati Rice by RiceTec in Alvin, Texas. It is a hybrid basmati rice strain grown in Texas. The rice is very aromatic and has a great taste, slightly reminiscent of nuts and grains. It's available in most supermarkets and comes packaged in nice, easy-to-measure-from plastic jars with tight-sealing lids to keep it fresh longer!

    1 dried ancho chile, seeds and veins removed
    2 Tbsp. olive oil
    1 small onion, chopped
    1 Tbsp. minced parsley
    1½ tsp. minced fresh thyme
    1½ cups long grain white rice
    2½ cups chicken stock
    ½ cup Shiner Bock beer
    1 tsp. minced lime zest
    Toasted sliced almonds as garnish

Place the ancho chiles in bowl of hot water; set aside for 15-20 minutes, or until chiles are soft and pliable. Coarsely chop the chiles and purée with a little of the water in which they soaked; set aside. Heat the olive oil in a heavy sauté pan over medium heat. When oil is hot, add the onion, parsley, and thyme. Sauté until onions are very wilted and lightly browned, about 5 minutes. Add the raw rice and cook, stirring often, to lightly brown the rice. Add the chicken stock, Shiner Bock, the reserved puréed chile and lime zest. Cook, covered, for about 30 minutes, or until rice is cooked through, but not overcooked. (It should not be sticky.) Garnish with toasted almonds and serve hot.

Index of Recipes

Lamb Chop Medallions on Creamy Spinach Gnocchi
with Shaved Parmesan, Port Wine Reduction
49-50

Lobster Rockefeller
7

Lobster Thermidor
30

Maple Black Peppercorn Buffalo Tenderloin
35

Oysters Rockefeller, Hôtel St. Germain
49

Oysters Texasfeller
11

Paulo's Salad
7

Pickled Black-Eyed Peas
30

Quail in Country Ham with Peppered Coffee
Gravy on Dirty Rice
80-81

Quail, Tequila Flamed, and Green Chili Cheese Grits
13-14

Quail, Wino
57

Red Beans and Rice Soup
18

Rice Pilaf, Shiner Bock
82

Roasted Garlic-Stuffed Beef Tenderloin with
Western Plaid Hash and Syrah Demi-glâce
44-45

Rock Shrimp Taquitos with Mango Barbecue
and Avocado Salsa
63-65

Salmon Ceviche with Capers,
Green Olives and Jalapeños
65

Shiner Bock Battered Soft Shell Crawfish
with Cilantro Orange Butter Sauce
43-44

Shiner Bock Rice Pilaf
82

Shrimp in Garlic Sauce (Camarones al Mojo de Ajo)
72-73

Shrimp (Rock) Taquitos with Mango Barbecue and Avocado Salsa
63-65

Sopa de Tortilla (Tortilla Soup)
72

Sourdough biscuits
25

Sourdough starter
25

Strawberries Romanoff
31

Tamale Tart with Roast Garlic Custard and Gulf Crabmeat
61-62

Tequila Flamed Quail & Green Chili Cheese Grits
13-14

Tex-Mex Spice
56

Tiramisu, Texas Port
8

Tissa's Dutch Oven Breakfast
24

Tortilla Soup
34-35

Venison Carpaccio with Green Peppercorn Dressing
13

White Chocolate and Pistachio Crême Brûlée
with Cherry Compote
51

White Rice (Arroz Blanco)
73

About the Author

JUDY ALTER IS THE AUTHOR OF NUMEROUS BOOKS, fiction and nonfiction, for adults and young adults. In recent years she has developed an interest in food writing, and her own cookbook/memoir, *Cooking My Way through Life: Kids and Books in the Kitchen*, will be released in 2009.

Great Texas Chefs

ISBN 978-0-87565-377-8
Case. $8.95

A TEXAS SMALL BOOK
★

Printed in China by Everbest through
Four Colour Imports, Ltd., Louisville, Kentucky

Design: Margie Adkins Graphic Design

ISBN 978-0-87565-377-8

5 0 8 9 5

9 780875 653778